SIX MONTHS
IN THE GOLD MINES;

FROM A JOURNAL OF

Three Years Residence

in
UPPER AND LOWER CALIFORNIA
1847-48-49.

BY
E. GOULD BUFFUM
LIEUTENANT FIRST REGIMENT NEW YORK VOLUNTEERS

PHILADELPHIA:
LEA AND BLANCHARD
1850

Unabridged reprint by
James Stevenson Publisher
Fairfield, California
707-469-0237
jimstevenson@jspub.com
http://www.jspub.com

Unabridged reprint
of Buffum's original book,
in new format and typeface,
and with new illustrations and cover
by
James Stevenson Publisher
October, 2000

Copyright©, 2000
by
James Stevenson Publisher
A derivative work
with new illustrations
All rights reserved

ISBN 1-885852-14-2
Library of Congress Card Number:
00-100529

Entered, according to Act of Congress, in the year 1850,
BY LEA AND BLANCHARD,

In the Clerk's Office of the District Court for the Eastern District of Pennsylvania.

PHILADELPHIA:

C. SHERMAN, PRINTER., 1850

TO

JOHN CHARLES FREMONT,

THE UNITED STATES SENATOR

FIRST CHOSEN TO REPRESENT
THE STATE OF CALIFORNIA

THE HISTORY
OF WHOSE INVALUABLE PIONEER LABOURS
WILL ENDURE AS LONG AS THE MOUNTAINS,
VALLEYS AND PLAINS
WHICH HIS COURAGE AND INDOMITABLE ENTERPRISE
EXPLORED,

AND HIS GENIUS HAS ILLUSTRATED,
THIS MEMORIAL
OF ADVENTURE,
BY PERMISSION,
IS MOST RESPECTFULLY INSCRIBED

BY
THE AUTHOR.

PUBLISHERS' NOTICE

Philadelphia, May 1850

THE pages of this work, in consequence of the public interest in all that appertains to California, have been hurried through the press, without the revision expected by the author; there may be, therefore, some slight errors detected through the pages. The writer of the work, formerly connected intimately with the New York press, has been a resident and explorer of California for more than three years, and still remains there. The proof sheets could not, therefore, well be submitted to his revision.

Fairfield, California, October 2000

TWO years ago, I spent a thoroughly enjoyable day in Coloma, California, at the site of the original mill, built by James W. Marshall for John Sutter. I spoke that day to one of the staff about diaries of miners. Mr. John Hutchinson, a gentleman who is well acquainted with both the locality and the history of the '49ers Gold Rush, directed my attention to this account of Edward Gould Buffum's travel and mining experiences. He and the others there clearly enjoy their work as they answer modern-day prospector's questions at the State Park Visitors' Center.

Buffum eloquently describes the countryside through which he passes, and gives early history that is not found in other sources. As a resident of Solano County, California, I was delighted to read his account of Suisun, which is adjacent to Fairfield, the Solano County seat, and of other locations around the state with which I am familiar. I am pleased to reintroduce Buffum's work at the sesquicentennial of the original publication of his noteworthy book.

James Stevenson, Ph.D.
Fairfield, California

PREFACE

In my work at the Gold Discovery Museum and Library in Coloma I have had the opportunity to read hundreds of California Gold Rush books. When publisher James Stevenson asked for my suggestions for future publications, Edward Gould Buffum's *Six Months in the Gold Mines* was the first to come to mind. Last published for public sale in 1966, it is long overdue for reprinting.

Buffum's occupation as soldier, miner and journalist in California from March of 1847 through 1851 put him in a position to record California's most important historic events. His intelligence, sensitivity and insight make it a first-class record.

Buffum wrote his book in 1850 for his Philadelphia publisher. It was also published in London the same year. Its intended audience was the reader hoping to strike it rich mining for gold and it served that readership well. Buffum described the birth of California as a state and foretold its great promise for the future.

Although Buffum's *Six Months in the Gold Mines* is not without its flaws, James Stevenson has wisely chosen to reproduce the text unedited. Now, 150 years after its first publication, today's reader has the opportunity to read and study one of the best eyewitness accounts of the Gold Rush and California's transformation into the 31st state.

John Hutchinson
Coloma, California

SIX MONTHS IN THE GOLD MINES

CONTENTS.

CHAPTER I.

Departure for the Mines—The Victims—Adventures of a Night on San Francisco Bay—Voyage in a Launch—My Companion Higgins—Resolutions of the Passengers—The Bay of San Pablo—The Straits of Carquinez—The Bay of Suisun—The Sacramento—Beautiful Scenery—Montezuma—Monte Diablo—Camp on Shore—Hala-chum-muck—Firing the Woods—Schwartz's Rancho—A "manifest destiny" Man—Involuntary Baptism—Sacramento City—The Embarcadero 21

CHAPTER II.

Arrival of our Party—The Mountaineer—A "prospecting Expedition—The Start—California Skies in November—A Drenching—Go-ahead Higgins — " Camp Beautiful — John the Irishman — The Indian's Grave—A "rock" Speech—The Return—Herd of Antelope—Johnson's Rancho—Acorn Gathering—Indian Squaws -Novel Costume -The Rancheria—Pule-u-le—A Bear Fight 27

CHAPTER III.

Yuba River—A Clean Shirt an Expensive Luxury—Yankee Pedler— The Upper and Lower Diggings—Foster's Bar—The Gold-Rocker—Gold-Digging and Gold-Washing—Return to the Embarcadero—Captain John A. Butter—Curious Currency—Sutter's Fort—Sam Brannan, and Co.—Washing Clothes—Salmon Shooting—Green Springs—Weaver's Creek—A Teamster's Bill 37

CHAPTER IV.

Our Log Cabin—Pi-pita-tua—Increase of our Party—The Dry Diggings of Weaver's Creek—The "Pockets" and "Nests" —Theory of the Gold Region—My First Day's Labour in the Placer—Extravagant Reports from the Middle Fork—Start for Culoma — Approach of

INTRODUCTION

the Rainy Season—The "Devil's Punch-Bowl"............ 45

CHAPTER V.

Sutter's Mill—Discovery of the Placers-Marshall and Bennett—Great Excitement—Desertion of the Pueblos and general Rush for the Mines-Gold-Mine Prices-Descent into a Canon—Banks of the Middle Fork—Pan Washing—Good Luck—Our Camp—Terrific Rain Storm—Sudden Rise of the River .... .51

CHAPTER VI.

Mormon Exploration of the Middle Fork—Headquarters of the Gold-hunters-The North Fork—Smith's Bar—Damming—Great Luck of a Frenchman and his Son—Kelsey's Bar—Rise and Fall of the Rivers---Return to Weaver's Creek — Agricultural Prospects — Culoma Sawmill—An Extensive and Expensive Breakfast— Prospecting on the South Fork—Winter Quarters —Snow-storm—A Robbery—Summary Justice—Garcia, Bissi, and Manuel—Lynch Law—Trial for attempt to Murder—Execution of the Accused—Fine Weather—How the Gold became distributed—Volcanic Crater 59

CHAPTER VII.

Monotonous Life at Weaver's Creek—Dry Diggings Uncertain—Discovery of a Rich Ravine—Great Results of One Day's Labour—Invasion of my Ravine-Weber and Dalor—The Indian Mode of Trading—A Mystery—Settlement of Weaverville—Price of Gold dust in the Winter of 1848—Gambling——Cost of Provisions—Opening of the Spring—Big Bar—Attack of the Land Scurvy—Symptoms and Treatment—Lucky Discovery—Progress of Culoma—Arrival of the First Steamer—Broadway Dandies wielding Pick and Shovel—Indian Outrages—Capture and Execution of Redskins. .
.... 67

SIX MONTHS IN THE GOLD MINES

CHAPTER VIII.

Extent and Richness of the Gold Region of Upper California—Are the "Gold-washings" inexhaustible ?—A Home for the Starving Millions of Europe and the Labouring Men of America—Suicidal Policy of our Military Governors—Union of Capital, Labour, and Skill—A Word to Capitalists—Joint-stock Companies—The Gold-bearing Quartz of the Sierra— Experience of Hon. G. W. Wright—Extraordinary Results of pulverizing Quartz Rock—The Gold Mines of Georgia—Steam Engines and Stamping Machines—Growth of Sacramento and San Francisco 77

CHAPTER IX.

The Mexican System of Government—Establishment of the Legislative Assembly of San Francisco-Seizure of the Town Records—Address of the Assembly recommending the Formation of a State Government —Interference of Brevet Brigadier-General Riley—Public Meeting— Organization of the State Convention—The Constitution — The Elections 85

CHAPTER X.

Growth of San Francisco—Number of Houses erected—Prices of Real Estate — Rents — Wages of Mechanics and Labourers—Gambling—Prices Current Climate—Churches—Steamboats—Statistics of Shipping, &c., &c., &c., ... 91

CHAPTER XI.

Weber—Sullivan- Stockton— Hudson—Georgetown— Sam Riper— The Slate Range—The "Biggest Lump yet found in California . . . .
. 95

CHAPTER XII.

Recapitulation—Population of the Mining Region—Average Amount of

8

INTRODUCTION

Gold Dug—Requirements of a Gold-Digger—The Best Season—In what kind of Soil is Gold Found ?—Washing Machines— California a Habitable Country—The Learned Professions 99

CHAPTER XIII.

The Old Towns of California 105

CHAPTER XIV

The New Towns of California 111

CHAPTER XV.

Lower California 119

Illustrations

The launch "Ann" 19

Camp Beautiful 36

Dry Diggings 50

Map of Gold Mining Region 58

Discovery of a rich ravine 76

Portsmouth Square, site of mass meetings in 1849 84

State Capitol at San Jose 90

Using a rocker to wash gold 104

Robert Semple, a proprietor of Benicia 117

Thomas O. Larkin, a proprietor of Benicia 118

INTRODUCTION

ON the 26th day of September, 1846, the 7th Regiment of New York State Volunteers, commanded by Colonel J. D. Stevenson, sailed from the harbour of New York under orders from the Secretary of War, to proceed to Upper California. The objects and operations of the expedition, the fitting out of which created some sensation at the time, are now too well understood and appreciated to require explanation. This regiment, in which I had the honour of holding a lieutenant's commission, numbered, rank and file, about seven hundred and twenty men, and sailed from New York in the ships Loo Choo, Susan Drew, and Thomas H. Perkins. After a fine passage of little more than five months, during which we spent several days pleasantly in Rio Janeiro, the Thomas H. Perkins entered the harbour of San Francisco and anchored off the site of the town, then called Yerba Buena, on the 6th day of March, 1847. The remaining ships arrived soon afterwards.

Alta California we found in quiet possession of the American land and naval forces—the "stars and stripes" floating over the old Mexican *presidios*. There being no immediate service to perform, our regiment was posted in small detachments through the various towns.

The now famous city of San Francisco, situated near the extreme end of a long and barren peninsular tract of land which separates the bay of San Francisco from the ocean, when first I landed on its beach was almost a solitude, there being not more than twelve or fifteen rough houses, and a few temporary buildings for hides, to relieve the view. Where now stands the great commercial metropolis of the Pacific, with its thirty thousand inhabitants, its busy streets alive with the hum of trade, were *corrals* for cattle and unoccupied sandy hills.

With the discovery of the gold mines, a new era in the history of California commences. This event has already changed a comparative wilderness into a flourishing State, and is destined to affect the commercial and political relations of the world. Between California as she was at the period of the cession to the United States and as she is at this time, there is no similitude. In two short years her mineral resources have been developed, and she has at once emerged from obscurity into a cynosure upon which nations are gazing with wondering eyes. Her mountains and valleys, but recently the hunting grounds of naked savages, are now peopled with a hundred thousand civilized men; her magnificent harbours crowded with ships from far distant ports; her rivers and bays navigated by steamboats; her warehouses filled with the products of almost every clime, and her population energetic, hopeful, and prosperous.

Although a history of California as she was would convey an entirely false idea of California as she is, it may not be amiss to look back a few months and see whence has sprung the young giantess now claiming admission on equal terms among the starry sisterhood of our Union.

Prior to the discovery of the *placers* the country was thinly peopled, the inhabitants being mostly native Californians, Mexicans, and Indians. The better classes lived the indolent life of *rancheros;* their wealth consisting in immense herds of cattle and horses running wild upon the hills and plains. The Indians, with the exception of those living in a wholly savage state, were little better than serfs, and performed all the drudgery and labour. The great staples and principal articles of trade were hides and tallow, for which goods at enormous prices were taken in exchange. Money was the scarcest article on the coast, many persons never seeing a dollar from one year's end to another, ox hides having acquired the name and answering the purpose of "California bank notes." The amusements of the country were gambling and *fandangoes,* freely participated in by both sexes, and all classes of the community. A few American, English, and French merchants resided at San Francisco, Monterey, Santa Barbara, and Los Angelos, who conducted the whole mercantile business of the country. The missions, once flourishing establishments, stripped of their privileges by the Mexican government, had fallen to decay. The native inhabitants, a kind, hospitable, and light-hearted race, too indolent even to desire more than an *adobe* house for a dwelling, beef and *frijoles* for food, and spirited horses to bear them dashingly over the hills and prairies, were either the victims of the tyranny of the central government, or of *pronunciamentos* and petty civil broils; and California, with her delicious climate, her inexhaustible resources, and important geographical position, might to this day have remained an almost unknown region; visited occasionally by a trading vessel with an assorted cargo, to be exchanged for hides, had not a mysterious Providence ordained the discovery of the golden sands of the Rio Americano. This event at once gave a tremendous impetus to commerce and emigration, and may be said to mark an important era in the history of the world.

Upper California, as defined by the old maps, embraces the region of

INTRODUCTION

country lying between the Rocky Mountains and the Sierra de los Mibres on the east, and the Pacific Ocean on the west; and is bounded on the north by the 42d degree of latitude, and on the south by *Baja* or Lower California and Sonora. Its extent from east to west is from six to seven hundred miles, with an area of about four hundred thousand square miles.

The boundaries of the new "State of California" as fixed by the Constitution are as follows, viz.: "Commencing at the point of intersection of the 42d degree of north latitude with the 120th degree of longitude west from Greenwich, and running south on the line of said 120th degree of west longitude until it intersects the 39th degree of north latitude; thence running in a straight line in a south-easterly direction to the river Colorado, at a point where it intersects the 35th degree of north latitude; thence down the middle of the channel of said river, to the boundary line between the United States and Mexico, as established by the treaty of May 30, 1848; thence running west and along said boundary line to the Pacific Ocean, and extending therein three English miles; thence running in a northwesterly direction, and following the Pacific coast to the 42d degree of north latitude; thence on the line of said 42d degree of north latitude to the place of beginning. Also all the islands, harbours, and bays, along and adjacent to the Pacific coast."

The new state, embracing the whole country between the Pacific and the 120th degree of west longitude, includes both the western and eastern flanks of the Sierra, and must contain an area of at least one hundred and fifty thousand square miles, being from one hundred to two hundred and fifty miles wide. This has been called the Maritime Region of California, and contains nearly all the territory susceptible of cultivation and inhabitable by civilized man. While the Great Basin or Desert lying east of the Sierra Nevada, between four and five thousand feet above the level of the sea, hemmed in on all sides by lofty ranges of snow-clad mountains, completely isolated and shut out from communication with any other part of the world for at least half the year, abounding in sterile plains and arid waters, with few fertile spots, must for ever remain a sparsely peopled region; the country lying west of the Sierra is smiling with plenty, and capable of sustaining a population of several millions.

There have never been greater mistakes made by writers than in describing and estimating the climate and resources of California. The most contradictory statements have been made, only to be reconciled on the ground that the country was seen from different points, and at different seasons of the year. It seems to have been forgotten that Upper California embraces a region of country extending along the coast of the Pacific a distance of more than six hundred miles, with a difference of ten degrees of latitude, affording scope for a wide range and vast difference of climate. The whole surface of the country is broken up into mountains, valleys and plains, and is traversed from north to south by the Sierra Nevada and the Coast Range, some of the volcanic peaks of the former rising to the height of sixteen thousand feet into the region of perpetual snow. The country directly bordering the coast has a high mean temperature, while a few miles interior the climate will be found of the mildest and most genial character—the atmosphere being remarkable for its softness and, purity. Taking a general view, I doubt much if any country in the world can boast a more equable and salubrious climate. South of Sutter's Fort, snow or ice is seldom or never seen, except in the dim distance on the crests of the mountain ranges. Upon the coast strong winds and fog prevail the greater part of the year, rendering it unpleasant, though by no means unhealthy. The appearance of the native population bears evidence to the salubrity of the climate. The men are tall, well formed, and robust, and when visiting their mother country, Mexico, have been looked upon almost as giants. The women are queenly, with dark, flashing eyes, and magnificent busts, and are remarkable for their fruitfulness. Families boasting twelve, fifteen, and even twenty-five children, have been frequently met with. With the exception of the new country now occupied by the miners, epidemics are unknown; and it is a singular fact, that that awful scourge of mankind, the cholera, has never left its destroying footprints in California. The great peculiarity of the climate is its rainy season. From the month of April to November rain is almost unknown, while during the winter months it falls in torrents. During the present season the rains, however, have been light, and delightful spring weather for a week or ten days successively has not been infrequent. During the "dry season, heavy night dews almost supply the place of rain, leaving the ground richly moistened in the morning.

The soil of California, like the face of the country, is extremely diversified. The hills are usually barren; while throughout the whole territory are well-watered valleys, whose soil is a rich black loam, capable of producing many of the tropical fruits, and all the products of the temperate zones. I cannot say I consider California, in its present condition, an agricultural

INTRODUCTION

country. The rich and extensive valleys which exist from north to south are indeed susceptible of the highest cultivation, and will produce in the greatest luxuriance, but the hills along the Coast Range are generally barren and sandy, and almost devoid of shrubbery, while the plains, during eight months of the year, are parched with the summer heat. There is this to be said, however ;—the experiment has never been fairly tried. When the mineral region shall offer less temptation than at present, and American industry and ingenuity have been brought to bear, the capacities of the soil will be fairly tested. The extensive and fertile valleys of the Sacramento and San Joaquin, which offer the greatest inducements to the agriculturist, lie north of San Francisco. The lower Sacramento valley is about one hundred and seventy miles long, and about sixty broad in the widest part. The valley of the San Joaquin is nearly three hundred miles long, and from fifty to sixty miles wide. Both of these valleys are well wooded, and are watered by the two great rivers (from which they take their name) and their tributaries, and abound with a great variety of game. Herds of elk, black-tailed deer, and antelopes are seen bounding over the hills and plains, — and grizzly bears, *coyotes,* minxes, badgers, hares, foxes, and wild geese are abundant. Wheat grows plentifully at many points yielding from thirty to fifty bushels to the acre. It is laid that much of the land will give an average yield of eighty bushels of wheat for every one sown.

The great difficulty in the way of extensive agricultural operations is the lack of rain. But wherever the soil can be irrigated, everything grows most luxuriantly; and it is astonishing to what an extent the wild oats and rye, which cover the Coast Range and some of the foot hills of the Sierra, grow even without it. In most places where the land can be irrigated, a succession of crops may be raised throughout the year. Water can always be found by digging for it, and the many small streams afford the means of irrigation.

South of San Francisco lie the beautiful and fertile valleys of San Jose and San Juan—the garden spot of California. In these valleys, and in the whole southern country below Point Conception and the *Cuesta de Santa Jues,* about latitude 35°, most of the tropical and all the fruits of the temperate zone are produced in great profusion. Figs, grapes, olives, bananas, pomegranates, peaches, apples, quinces, pears, melons, and plums of the finest quality grow abundantly. The olive of California is larger than the French, and declared by *gourmets* to be far superior in flavour,—while the wine pressed from the Californian grape needs only to become better known to be appreciated. Among the fruits of California growing wild throughout the whole country, is the *tuna* or prickly pear, one of the most delicious fruits I have eaten. Onions, potatoes, parsnips, carrots, and other culinary vegetables, are produced in the lower country in great size and abundance. Hemp grows wild in many places, and sugar-cane, cotton, and rice may be grown upon the plains with the aid of irrigation. There is no country in the world better adapted for grazing; and the raising of stock, particularly sheep, will yet prove one of the most profitable branches of industry. The wild shrubbery is of an excellent character for sheep, and the climate is peculiarly adapted to their growth.

In mineral resources California stands unrivalled. To say nothing at present of her immense *placers* of gold, she contains within her bosom minerals of other kinds sufficient to enrich her. In the north, on the Coast Range above Sonoma, saltpetre, copper, sulphur, and lead, have been found in large quantities; the latter so pure, that I was told by an old hunter two years ago, that he had frequently run his bullets from the ore. Silver mines have been discovered on the south side of San Francisco Bay, and near the *Pueblo de San Jose* are the famous quicksilver mines of New Almaden, said to be superior to those of Spain. A species of coal, between the bituminous and the anthracite, has been found in the vicinity of San Diego, San Luis Obispo, and Santa Cruz, and iron exists throughout the country.

California occupies a geographical position of the first rank and importance, and must eventually control the commerce of the vast Pacific. With a coast extending more than six hundred miles from north to south, indented with numerous bays and harbours, connected with her golden interior almost to the base of the lofty Sierra by navigable streams, blessed with a mild and salubrious climate, and capable of sustaining a large population, she must one day become the *entrepôt* of the commerce of the East. With South America on the one side and Oregon on the other— the vast empire of China, the rich isles of the Indies, Polynesia, Japan, and the Sandwich Islands, lying close at hand—a steam communication will connect her with the most distant of these points in a few weeks. When with iron hands she is connected with the great valley of the Mississippi, and thence with the shores of the Atlantic, the commerce which now is borne around Cape Horn must inevitably pass through her borders; and long ere that is accomplished, the completion of the railroad across the Isthmus of Panama, or a

INTRODUCTION

ship canal across that of Tehuantepec, will bind her with a closely woven chain to the eastern shores of our Union.

The following pages have been written *currente calamo,* in moments stolen from the cares of business, within sound of the click of hammers, the grating of saws, and all the noise, bustle, excitement, speculation, and confusion of San Francisco, and on the eve of my departure for a further exploration of the great southern mines. Under these circumstances, no particular regard has been paid to style. It is not to be expected that a California gold-hunter can afford to bestow hours on the mere polishing of sentences and rounding of periods like a Parisian *litterateur.* They contain a narrative of my journey to, and life and adventures in, the golden region of California, during the autumn, winter, and spring of 1848—9, with a full and complete description of the principal *placers,* the process of extracting gold from the earth, and the necessary machines and implements; a theory of the origin of the golden sands; an account of the gold-bearing quartz of the Sierra Nevada; a history of the rise and progress of the principal new towns and cities; the formation of the state government, and a six months' residence on the Gulf of Lower California. I have endeavoured to give a truthful narrative, and statistics upon which reliance may be placed, with a view to a better understanding of the subject than can be gained from the garbled, and in some cases maliciously untrue statements, which have flooded the eastern press, written in some cases by men who have never been farther than the town of San Francisco or Stockton, and who of course know nothing of the country or the *placers.*

The statements of one attracted to California by other charms than those of gold, a resident within her borders for nearly three years, conversant with the language, manners, and customs of her inhabitants, an observer of her wonderful growth, and a gold-digger for six months, will undoubtedly be received with consideration; and if I succeed in imparting to my readers (every one of whom has probably a brother or some dear friend here), a correct idea of this interesting region, to which the eyes of the whole world are now directed, I shall have achieved my object.

At the time of the discovery of the *placers,* I was stationed at La Paz, Lower California, but being ordered to Upper California, arrived at Monterey in the middle of June, 1848, about six weeks after the discovery had been made public. The most extravagant stories were then in circulation, but they were mostly viewed as the vagaries of a heated fancy by the good people of Monterey; I was ordered to the Pueblo de los Angelos for duty, where I arrived on the fourth day of July, and remained with the detachment with which I was connected until it was disbanded, on the 18th day of September, 1848. The day of our disbandment was hailed with joy such as a captive must feel on his release from slavery. For three long months we had anxiously awaited the event. The stories from the mines breathed the spirit of the Arabian tales, and visions of "big lumps" floated before our eyes. In three days *La Ciudad de los Angelos* was deserted by its former occupants, and wagons and horses laden with tin pans, crowbars, iron pots, shovels, pork, and pick axes, might have been seen on the road to the *placers*. On the 18th of October, I reached San Francisco, where curious state of things was presented. Gold dust and coin were plentiful as the sea-shore sands, and seemed to be thought about as valuable. The town had but little improved since I first saw it, as upon the discovery of the mines it had been nearly deserted by its inhabitants. Real estate had been slowly depreciating for several months, and the idea of San Francisco being a large city within two years had not yet been broached. Merchandise of all descriptions was exceedingly high. Flour was selling at $60 per barrel; dried beef 50 cents per pound; coffee 50 cents; shovels $10 each; tin pans $5 do.; crow-bars $10 do.; red flannel shirts $5 do.; common striped shirts $5 do.; common boots $16 per pair; and everything else in proportion. I made a few purchases and held myself in readiness to start for the placers.

San Francisco, January 1st, 1850.

INTRODUCTION

The "Ann" was a little launch....

SIX MONTHS IN THE GOLD MINES.

CHAPTER I.

Departure for the Mines—The Victim—Adventures of a Night on San Francisco Bay—Voyage in a Launch—My Companion Higgins—Resolutions of the Passengers—The Bay of San Pablo—The Straits of Carquinez—Benicia—The Bay of Suisun—The Sacramento—Beautiful Scenery—Montezuma—Monte Diablo—Camp on Shore—Hala-Chum-Muck—Firing the Woods—Schwartz's Rancho—A "manifest destiny" man—Involuntary Baptism—Sacramento City—The Embarcadero

ARMED with a pickaxe, shovel, hoe, and rifle, and accoutered in a red flannel shirt, corduroy pants, and heavy boots, and accompanied by two friends, I found myself, on the afternoon of the 25th of October, 1848, wending my way to the only wharf in San Francisco, to take passage for the golden hills of the Sierra Nevada. The scenes that for days had met my eyes, and even as I was stepping on board the launch, might have damped the ardour of a more adventurous man. Whole launch-loads of miserable victims of fever and ague were daily arriving from the mining region - sallow, weak, emaciated and dispirited but I had nerved myself for the combat, and doubt not that I would have taken passage when I did and as I did, had the arch-enemy of mankind himself stood helmsman on the little craft that was to bear me to El Dorado. We had engaged and paid our passage, and such was our eagerness to get a conveyance of some kind, that we had not even looked at the frail bark in which we were to entrust our now more than ever before valuable bodies.

The "Ann" was a little launch of about ten tons burden, a mere ship's boat, entirely open, and filled with barrels and merchandise of every kind, and eight human beings, who, besides ourselves, had taken passage in her. I looked at her, there was not room upon her deckless hull to stow a brandy bottle securely. We tried to reason the captain into an idea of the danger of proceeding with so much freight, but the only reply he gave us was, that he received four dollars a hundred for it. There was no alternative, so in we jumped, and about dusk the boat was under way, and scudding with a fair wind across the bay of San Francisco.

There was, of course; no room to cook on board, and there was no galley or furnace to cook in; and, indeed, there was nothing to cook, as in our hurry we had neglected to make purchases of any necessary articles of food, and expected to be furnished with our meals among the other accommodations of our boat. The captain generously offered us some cheese and crackers, and after regaining ourselves on these, we commenced instituting a search for sleeping-places. It was by this time dark, and black clouds were sweeping over the sky. The wind had changed, and we were beating off and on Angel Island, while the spray was dashing over our boats sides, which were nearly level with the water from her great load. It augured anything but a pleasant night, and here were eleven of us, with a prospect of rain and spray, forced to find some means of sleeping on the pile of barrels or boxes that loaded the boat, or pass a night of sleeplessness.

Sharper-sighted than my companion, I had spied out a box of goods lying aft that rose above the mingled mass around it, and upon which, by doubling myself into a most unnatural and ungentlemanly position, I could repose the upper portion of my body, while my heels rested on the chines of a pork-barrel, at an angle of about forty-five degrees above my head. With a selfishness peculiar to the human race, I appropriated the whole of this couch to myself, and was already in the land of dreams, with bright visions of big lumps and bigger piles of gold flitting before my spiritual eyes, when I felt myself roughly shaken, and awaking, found Higgins, one of my companions, standing at my side, who coolly informed me that "my time was up, and it was now his turn." It seems that, during my absence in the visionary world, a council had been held by all hands, in which it was gravely decided and resolved, *First*, "that there was no other feasible sleeping-place than the box then occupied by me;" *Secondly*, " that it was contrary to the laws of all human society, that one man should appropriate to his own private and individual use *all* of this worlds goods;" and *Thirdly*, "that, for the next twenty-four hours, all hands should in rotation take a nap upon the box." When Higgins woke me, the rain-drops were pattering upon my "serape," and half asleep I jumped up, and going forward, found a little place where I could half lie down; and in this manner, with the rain-drops and surf dashing upon me, and every roll of the little boat threatening to cast me upon

DEPARTURE FOR THE MINES

the waters, I passed that night on the bay of San Francisco, a night which I shall never forget. My companions and fellow-sufferers, when not occupying the box, were either catching an occasional wink in a perpendicular position, or sitting upon the chines of a barrel, wishing with all their hearts for daylight.

Morning at length came, as morning always will, even after the longest night, and the warm sun soon was shining upon us, and drying our wet clothing, and invigorating our dampened spirits. We had passed, during the night, out of the bay of San Francisco into that of San Pablo. This bay is about ten miles in diameter, its form being nearly circular. Its entrance is about eight miles from the town of San Francisco, and is marked by two rocky islands known as the Two Brothers, lying a few yards from each other, and white with bird lime. The usual channel is on the left of these rocks. From the bay of San Pablo we entered the straits of Carquinez, thirty-five miles from San Francisco, and at about noon we were abreast of the town of Benicia.

The straits of Carquinez are about one mile in width, and six in length, and connect the bay of San Pablo with that of Suisun. Near the head of the straits and the entrance to Suisun Bay, is placed the city of Benicia. This town was the first laid out among the new towns of California, and many months before the discovery of the mines gave a tremendous impetus to town making. Benicia seems destined to become a great city, and perhaps rival San Francisco in point of commercial importance, possessing, as it unquestionably does, many advantages over it. The banks are bold and steep, and sufficient depth of water is found here at all seasons for vessels to lie and discharge their cargoes directly at the bank; while at San Francisco the tide only serves once in twenty-four hours, and even then all cargoes are obliged to be transported in launches and scows from the ships, which are forced to lie at some distance from the shore, in consequence of the broad flat in front of the town.

Leaving Benicia, we proceeded into the bay of Suisun, and passing the delta of the San Joaquin, entered the magnificent Sacramento, the Hudson of the western world. The lofty Palisades are not here; but to the lover of the picturesque and beautiful, the tall oak groves, through which the deer, the elk, and antelope are bounding, the golden hue of the landscape, the snowy peaks of the distant Sierra, the lofty Mount Diablo, and the calm, broad, and placid river, present a scene upon the Sacramento as enchanting as that which broke upon the enraptured vision of old Hendrick Hudson. At the entrance of the river the land is low and somewhat marshy, being covered with a thick, rank growth of *tule*, a species of rush, of which the Indians make baskets, chairs, and many little articles. On the left bank of the entrance to the Sacramento was the magnificent city of Montezuma, consisting of one unfinished house, through which the autumn winds were rattling. This is one of the paper towns laid out some three years since, and abandoned since the discovery of the placers has brought out more favourable points of location. The Sacramento here is about a mile in width; and to the right, rising up apparently from the end of the tule prairie, is the rugged peak of Monte Diablo (Devils Mountain), four thousand feet in height. The low, alluvial bottom lands along the shore appear susceptible of the highest cultivation; and I doubt not, when the gold mania shall have partially ceased, the rich bottoms of the Sacramento will be clothed with farm-houses, the abodes of happiness, peace, and plenty, and that the music of lowing herds will resound over its spreading prairies.

At the mouth of the river there is very little timber; but in our progress upward we found the oak and the sycamore growing most luxuriantly; and, extending back on the left bank as far as the eye could reach, a spreading prairie of wild oats and mustard, the latter raising its yellow-flowered head to the height of many feet. We tied up for the night about four miles from the entrance of the river, and building a large fire on shore, and cooking some potatoes and pork, with which the captain generously furnished us, determining to spend this night stretched upon a level, went to sleep around the camp fire, and made good ere morning for our previous nights misery, and slept in utter disregard of the wolves and grizzly bears which abound in that region.

The next day, there being no wind, we were obliged to pull for it, and about dusk reached Hala-chum-muck, or, as it is now called, Suisun, a city under that cognomen having been laid out here. The "city" is on the left bank of the river, and about fifteen miles from its mouth, on a bold, high bank, and surrounded by a fine growth of oak timber. Hala-chum-muck is an old stopping-place on the river; and finding the remains of a house here, we tied up, and going on shore, and making a fire from the remnants of some, boards, which had been pulled from the roof of the house, cooked another supper, and slept on the ground, with a small piece of roof over our heads.

DEPARTURE FOR THE MINES

Hala-chum-muck derives its name from an Indian story connected with it. Many years ago, a party of hunters were encamped here for the night, and being attacked by Indians, after a brave resistance were all killed, with the exception of one, who, as he was escaping, was followed with a cry from the Indians of Hala-chum-muck (nothing to eat), probably, as he had been forced to throw down his rifle, signifying thereby that they would leave him to die of starvation. The spot has, ever since that time, borne the name of Hala-chum-muck.

There were three families living here, with a stock of cattle, when the placers were discovered, and Hala-chum-muck was bidding fair to be a town; but on the reception of the golden news, they deserted their ranchos, and the crews of launches which stopped here soon killed off the cattle and destroyed the dwellings. Lots in Suisun, however, are now selling rapidly, and at high rates.

We continued our progress up the river, occasionally stopping and amusing ourselves by firing the woods on either side, and watching the broad flames as they spread and crackled through the underbrush. On the night of the 30th, we hauled up at the rancho of Schwartz an old German, of whom Bryant speaks as a man who has forgotten his own language, and never acquired any other. He is certainly the most curious specimen of humanity it has ever my lot to witness. He emigrated to California some ten years since, and obtained a grant of six leagues of land, extending up and down the Sacramento River; and in the progress of time he will probably be one of the richest land-holders of California. He has built upon the bank of the river a little hut of tule, resembling an Indian wigwam; and there he lives, a "manifest destiny" man, with "masterly inactivity" awaiting the march of civilization, and anticipating at some future day the sale of his lands for a princely fortune, a hope in which he will probably not be disappointed. His language is a mixture of his old mother German, English, Spanish, French, and Indian; and it would require an apter linguist than it was ever my good fortune to meet with, to comprehend his "lingua."

I underwent an operation at Schwartz's rancho, that sealed my full connexion and communion with the region to which I was travelling. It was no less than an impromptu baptism in the golden waters of the Sacramento. We had built a fire on shore, and having purchased from Schwartz a few pounds of beef at gold-diggers prices, i.e. one dollar per pound, had eaten our supper, when I started for the launch which lay about ten yards from the shore, to get my blankets. The only conveyance was an old log canoe of Schwartz's; and seating myself in it, in company with one of my companions and an Indian boy he had brought with him, we pushed off. The Indian was seated in the canoe's bow, and was frightened by the oscillating motion given to it, when it was first pushed off from the shore. To balance the roll upon one side, he leaned to the other, and finding a corresponding motion in that direction, he reversed his position, and leaning too far, upset the canoe, and all three of us. I, with a heavy overcoat on, and my rifle in hand, tumbled into about fifteen feet of water. I dropped the rifle as though it were boiling lead, and made the best of my way to the shore. We all arrived safely on terra firma, and going on board alone in the canoe, I changed my clothing. Telling old Schwartz that I must encroach upon his hospitality, and drinking about a pint of some coloured New England rum, which he assured me was "de tres best clasa de brandy," I stretched my blankets on the mud floor of his wigwam, and awoke in the morning in as good health and spirits as though nothing had happened. I engaged the services of a Kanaka, who was on board, to dive for my rifle; and after he had brought it up, we got under way, and after sleeping another night on the banks of the Sacramento, reached the Embarcadero, now Sacramento City, on the evening of November 2d. The river here is about eight hundred feet wide.

The beautiful plain on which is now located the thriving and populous city of Sacramento, was, when I first landed there, untenanted. There was not a house upon it, the only place of business being an old store-ship laid up upon its bank. Where now, after a lapse of only one year, a flourishing city with a population of twelve thousand stands, I pitched my tent on the edge of a broad prairie.

To complete the party with which we intended going to the mines, we were obliged to wait at the Embarcadero for three of our disbanded soldiers, who had left the Pueblo de los Angeles about the time we did, and were coming by land through the Tulare valley, as we required their horses to pack the provisions we had brought with us.

We pitched our tent, cooked our provisions, and anxiously waited the arrival of the men, a prey to the greatest excitement, continually hearing as we did, the most extravagant stories from the mining region. The intense heat of the summer solstice had given way to autumns cooling breezes, and parties were daily arriving at and leaving the Embarcadero; the former with their pockets well lined with gold dust, and the latter with high hopes and beating hearts.

CHAPTER II.

Arrival of our Party—The Mountaineer—A "prospecting" Expedition—The Start —California Skies in November —A Drenching—Go-ahead Higgins—Camp Beautiful— John the Irishman—The Indian's Grave— A "rock" Speech— The Return—Herd of Antelope— Johnson Rancho —Acorn Gathering—Indian Squaws—Novel Costume—The Rancheria—Pule-u-le—A Bear Fight.

ON the 7th of November our party arrived, their horses, of which they brought five, jaded with the travel in the mountains; and it was not until the 16th that we were able to make a start. Being, of course, entirely ignorant of the best locality to which to proceed, and being all young, strong, and enthusiastic, we determined to strike out a new path, and go on an exploring expedition in the mountains, in the hope that fortune would throw in our way the biggest of all lumps, and that we might possibly find the fountainhead of El Dorado, where, gushing in a rich and golden lava from the heart of the great Sierra, a stream of molten gold should appear before our enraptured eyes.

Fortune, or rather misfortune, favoured us in this project. We were visited one evening in camp by a man, who informed us that he had recently been on a "prospecting" expedition with a party of three others, and that after nearly reaching, as he thought, the fountain head of gold, the party was attacked by Indians, and all, with the exception of himself killed. The prospect, he told us, was most favourable, and learning from him the direction of the mountains in which he had been, with two pack-horses lightly laden with hard bread and dried beef, six of us started on the evening of November 16th on our Quixotic expedition, leaving one with the remainder of our provisions and the tent at the Embarcadero.

We crossed the Rio de los Americanos about a mile above Sutter's Fort, and, encamping upon its opposite bank, started on the morning of the 17th. The sky promised a heavy rain storm; nothing daunted, however, we pushed in the direction of the Bear River settlements, and about noon the sky's predictions were most fully realized. The rain fell in big drops, and soon broke upon us in torrents. The wind blew a hurricane, and we were in the apparent centre of an open prairie, with a row of sheltering trees about four miles distant, mockingly beckoning us to seek protection beneath their thick and wide-spreading branches.

We pushed on, and succeeded in reaching the trees which proved to be evergreen oaks, in a little more than an hour, wet to the skin. The little clothing we had brought with us, and packed upon the horses backs, was also wet, and our bread reduced to the consistency of paste. We were dispirited, but managed to build a fire beneath the trees, and remained there throughout the day. The rain ceased at nightfall, and making a sorry supper from our wet bread and slimy meat, we stretched ourselves on the ground, wrapped in our blankets, heartily cursing our folly in travelling out of the beaten track with the hopes of rendering ourselves rich and our names immortal. But tired men will sleep even in wet blankets and on muddy ground and we were half compensated in the morning for our previous days adventures and misfortunes by as bright a sunshine and clear a sky as ever broke upon a prairie. Gathering up our provisions we made a start for the purpose of reaching, before night set in, a ravine where we were, according to our directions, to leave the main road and strike for the mountains.

About dusk we reached a dry "arroyo," which we supposed to be the one indicated on the rough draft of the road we were to travel, given us by the mountaineer who had first impressed our minds with the idea of this expedition. We unpacked, built a roaring fire in the centre of the arroyo, and placing our wet bread and beef in its immediate vicinity, had them soon in a fair way of drying. We lay down again at night, with a bright starlit sky resting peacefully over us, and hoped for an invigorating rest; but California skies in November are not to be trusted, and so we found to our sorrow, for about twelve o'clock we were all turned out by a tremendous shower of rain. We gathered around the expiring fire, and our sorrows for our bodily sufferings were all soon absorbed in the thought that there lay our poor bread and meat, our sole dependence for support, once half dried and now suffering a second soaking. There being no indications of a cessation of the rain, we stretched over our provisions a small tent we had brought with us, and for not having previously pitched which we cursed ourselves heartily, and spent the remainder of the night in sleeplessness and wet.

The tantalizing morning again broke fair, and it was decided to remain where we were throughout the day, and make another attempt at drying our provisions, and at the same time fully decide what to do. Two of the party (myself included) wished either to turn back and try some other part of the digging, or proceed on the main road which we bad been

ARRIVAL OF OUR PARTY

travelling, and near which we were then encamped, directly to the Yuba River, at a distance, as we supposed, of about thirty miles. But the go-ahead party was too powerful for us, and, headed by Higgins, a man of the most indomitable perseverance, pictured to us the glorious results we were to achieve. We were to go where the track of the white man was yet unseen, and find in the mountain's stony heart a home for the winter, with untold riches lying beneath our feet. We yielded, and the next morning at daylight started again, making a straight course for the mountains, lying in a northeasterly direction, and apparently about twenty-five miles distant. And here we were, started on an unknown track, to go among hostile savages, who we knew had already killed our countrymen, our provisions for six consisting of about twenty-five pounds of wet and already moulded hard bread and some miserable jerked beef.

We travelled up the "arroyo" till nearly sunset, when we struck the foot-hills of the mountains. We had seen no foot-tracks, except an occasional naked one of an Indian, and I became fully satisfied that we had taken the wrong arroyo as our diverging point. The ground over which we had travelled that day was a miserable stony soil, with here and there a scrubby oak tree growing. As we struck the foot of the mountains the scene was changed. Rich, verdant, and fertile-looking valleys opened out before us, and tall oaks threw a luxuriant, lengthened evening shadow upon the gentle slope of their ascent. We entered the midst of these valleys, and, after proceeding nearly a mile, came to the prettiest camping spot I ever saw. An expansion of the valley formed a circular plain of about a mile in diameter, surrounded on all sides, excepting at its one narrow entrance, with green, tree-covered, and lofty hills. A tall growth of grass and wild oats, interspersed with beautiful blue and yellow autumnal flowers, covered the plain, and meandering through it, with a thousand windings, was a silvery stream, clear as crystal, from which we and our thirsty horses drank our fill, and relished the draught, I believe, better than the gods ever did their nectar. It was a beautiful scene. The sun was just sinking behind the hills on the western side, and threw a golden stream of light on the opposite slope. Birds of gaudy plumage were carolling their thousand varied notes on the tree branches, and I thought if gold and its allurements could be banished from my thoughts, I could come here and live in this little earthly paradise happily for ever.

We selected a gentle slope, beneath a huge rock, near the western hill-side, for our camping ground, and, again building a fire, were about to content ourselves with a supper of mouldy bread, when a jolly son of the Emerald Isle who was one of our party, in diving among the little bags of which our packs consisted, found one of burnt and ground coffee, which we did not know we possessed, and another of sugar, both to be sure a little wet, but nevertheless welcome. Talk of the delights of sipping the decoction of the brown berry after a hearty dinner at "Delmonico's"! That dish of hot coffee, drunk out of my quart tin pot, in which also I had boiled it, was a more luxurious beverage to me than the dew-drops in a new-blown rose could be to a fairy. I slept delightfully under its influence till midnight, when I was called to stand my turn of guard duty, which, as we were in an Indian region, all knew to be necessary; and I, who so often with my sword belted around me, had commanded guard as their officer, watched post with my old rifle for nearly two hours.

The day broke as clear and beautiful upon our enchanting valley as the previous one had closed. After partaking of another pot of hot coffee and some mouldy bread, I took a stroll across the little stream, with my rifle for my companion, while the others, more enthusiastic, started in search of gold. I crossed the plain, and found, at the foot of the hill on the other side, a deserted Indian hut, built of bushes and mud. The fire was still burning on the mud hearth, a few gourds filled with water were lying at the entrance, and an ugly dog was growling near it. Within a few feet of the hut was a little circular mound enclosed with a brush paling. It was an Indians grave, and placed in its centre, as a tombstone, was a long stick stained with a red colouring, which also covered the surface of the mound. Some proud chieftain probably rested here, and as the hut bore evident marks of having been very recently deserted, his descendants had without doubt left his bones to moulder there alone, and fled at the sight of the white man.

Leaving this spot, I returned to camp, and, as the gold-hunters had not yet come back, still continued to stroll around it. The top of the rock beneath which we had slept was covered with deep and regularly made holes, like those found in the rocks where rapids of rivers have fallen for centuries and worn them out. It was long before I could account for the existence of these, but finally imagined, what I afterwards found to be the fact, that they were made by the continual pounding of the Indians in mashing their acorns. In the vicinity I observed several groves of a species of white oak (Quercus longiglanda), some of them eight feet in diameter, and at least eighty feet high. This tree is remarkable for the length of its acorns, several

ARRIVAL OF OUR PARTY

that I picked up measuring two inches.

The gold-hunters finally returned, and with elongated countenances reported that, though they had diligently searched every little ravine around our camp, the nearest they could come to gold-finding was some beautiful specimens of mica, which John the Irishman brought in with him, insisting that it was pure "gold. We camped again in the valley that night, and the next morning held another council as to what we should do and whither we should go. Higgins, as usual, was for going ahead; I was for backing out; and the little party formed itself into two factions, Higgins at the head of one, and I of the other. Mounting the rock, I made not exactly a "stump," but a "rock" speech, in which, to my own satisfaction, and, as it proved, to that of the majority of the party, I explained the madness of the idea of starting into the mountains on foot, without a guide, and with but about two or three days provisions remaining. We had seen but few deer so far, and knew not whether there were any in the mountains. I recommended that we should immediately pack up, and strike what we thought to be the best course for Johnson's Rancho, on Bear River, about fifteen miles from Yuba. I succeeded, and we packed up and retraced our steps, with somewhat heavy hearts, down the little valley. We left our blessing on the lovely spot, named our camping ground Camp Beautiful, and proceeded on our way, following the base of the mountains. There was no road, and we knew not whither we were going, only that we were in the right direction. The country outside of the mountains was miserably poor and barren, the soil being covered with a rocky flint. It is entirely destitute of timber, excepting on the banks of the arroyos, which were then dry, and are all skirted with magnificent ever-green oaks. We were travelling in a northwesterly direction, and hoped to reach Bear River at night; coming, however, to a little stream we camped upon its margin, and the next day started again, refreshed by a good nights sleep, but dispirited from our ignorance of where we were, or whither we were going, besides being foot-sore from our travel over the flinty pebbles. About noon we saw, at a distance of some three or four miles, an immense flock of what we took to be sheep. Elated at the prospect of being near a rancho, we speedily unpacked a horse, and using the pack lashing for a bridle, I mounted him, and galloped at full speed in the direction of the flock, hoping to find the rancho to which they belonged near them. I approached to within three hundred yards of them before I discovered the mistake under which I had laboured, when the whole herd went bounding away affrighted. What I had taken for a flock of sheep was a herd of antelope; containing, I should suppose, nearly a thousand, and for a supper of one of which I would have freely given a months anticipated labour in the gold mines. I returned to the party, and dampened their already disheartened spirits by my report.

We travelled on slowly, for we were wearied and heart-sick, and at about four o'clock in the afternoon, having traversed a very circuitous route, the horses were unpacked and the small quantity of remaining provisions put in our pockets. Higgins, the owner of one of the horses, mounted his, and John the Irishman, who was suffering with a rheumatic complaint, the other. I was so weary and weak that I could scarcely support myself, and my feet were so covered with blisters, and so swollen, that every step I took seemed like treading on sharpened spikes. How I wished myself back in Camp Beautiful, in Texas, anywhere but where I was. I was lagging behind the party, when John, turning round, saw me, and stopped his horse; as I came up to him he dismounted and forced me to take his place. God bless thee! generous Irishman. Beneath a rough exterior he had a heart which beat with feelings and emotions to which many a proud bosom is a stranger. How I loaded him with thanks, and only received his unsophisticated reply, that I "was tireder than he was." About dark we struck a stream of water, and all but Higgins were ready and glad to camp and eat the last remains of the mouldy bread and beef. The persevering energy of Higgins had not in the least degree failed him, and without getting off his horse, he bade us good-bye, and assured us that he would never return till he had found Johnson's Rancho. He left us: we built up a good fire, and about three hours afterward, while speculating on his return, he came dashing into camp with about a dozen pounds of fresh beef, some bread, and a bottle of fine old brandy. We welcomed him as we would an angel visitant. My distaste for his desperation changed into an admiration for his energy. It seems he had found a road about forty yards from our camp, and a ride of five miles had brought him to Johnson's Rancho. We made a good supper of beef and bread, and revived our fainting spirits with the brandy, and in the fulness of our hearts unanimously voted Higgins excused from guard duty for that night. Next morning, light-hearted and happy, we started for the rancho, and crossing Bear River, on which it is situated, reached there about ten o'clock. Johnson is an American, who many years since obtained a large grant of fertile land on Bear River, and has been living here for years within fifteen miles of a stream

ARRIVAL OF OUR PARTY

whose banks and bed were filled with incalculable riches.

We procured some provisions here, and started for the Yuba, and without any mishaps reached the camping ground, about three miles from the river, early in the afternoon. We camped, and Higgins and myself started on a hunting expedition, for the purpose of getting some game for supper. We made our way into the hills, and were travelling slowly, trailing our rifles, when we stopped suddenly, dumbfounded, before two of the most curious and uncouth-looking objects that ever crossed my sight. They were two Indian women, engaged in gathering acorns. They were entirely naked, with the exception of a *coyote* skin extending from the waists to the knees. Their heads were shaved, and the tops of them covered with a black tarry paint, and a huge pair of military whiskers were daubed on their cheeks with the same article. They had with them two conical-shaped wicker baskets, in which they were placing the acorns, which were scattered ankle deep around them. Higgins, with more gallantry than myself, essayed a conversation with them, but made a signal failure, as after listening to a few sentences in Spanish and English, they seized their acorn baskets and ran. The glimpse we had taken of these mountain beauties, and our failure to enter into any conversation with them, determined us to pay a visit to their headquarters, which we knew were near by. Watching their footsteps in their rapid flight, we saw them, after descending a hill, turn up a ravine, and disappear. We followed in the direction which they had taken, and soon reached the Indian rancheria. It was located on both sides of a deep ravine, across which was thrown a large log as a bridge, and consisted of about twenty circular wigwams, built of brush, plastered with mud, and capable of containing three or four persons. As we entered, we observed our flying beauties, seated on the ground, pounding acorns on a large rock indented with holes similar to those which so puzzled me at Camp Beautiful. We were suddenly surrounded upon our entrance by thirty or forty male Indians, entirely naked, who had their bows and quivers slung over their shoulders, and who stared most suspiciously at us and our rifles. Finding one of them who spoke Spanish, I entered into a conversation with him told him we had only come to pay a visit to the rancheria and, as a token of peace offering, gave him about two pounds of musty bread and some tobacco which I happened to have in my game-bag. This pleased him highly, and from that moment till we left, *Pule-u-le*, as he informed me his name was, appeared my most intimate and sworn friend. I apologized to him for the unfortunate fright which we had caused a portion of his household, and assured him that no harm was intended, as I entertained the greatest respect for the ladies of his tribe, whom I considered far superior in point of ornament, taste, and natural beauty to those of any other race of Indians in the country. Pule-u-le exhibited to me the interior of several of the wigwams, which were nicely thatched with sprigs of pine and cypress, while a matting of the same material covered the bottom. During our presence our two female attractions had retired into one of the wigwams, into which Pule-u-le piloted us, where I found some four or five squaws similarly bepitched and clothed, and who appeared exceedingly frightened at our entrance. But Pule-u-le explained that we were friends, and mentioned the high estimation in which I held them, which so pleased them that one of the runaways left the wigwam and soon brought me in a large piece of bread made of acorns, which to my taste was of a much more excellent flavour than musty hard bread.

Pule-u-le showed us the bows and arrows, and never have I seen more beautiful specimens of workmanship. The bows were some three feet long, but very elastic and some of them beautifully carved, and strung with the intestines of birds. The arrows were about eighteen inches in length, accurately feathered, and headed with a perfectly clear and transparent green crystal, of a kind which I had never before seen, notched on the sides, and sharp as a needle at the point. The arrows, of which each Indian had at least twenty, were carried in a quiver made of coyote skin.

I asked Pule-u-le if he had ever known of the existence of gold prior to the entrance of white men into the mines. His reply was that, where he was born, about forty miles higher up the river, he had, when a boy, picked it from rocks in large pieces, and amused himself by throwing them into the river as he would pebbles. A portion of the tribe go daily to the Yuba River, and wash out a sufficient amount of gold to purchase a few pounds of flour, or some sweetmeats, and return to the *rancheria* at night to share it with their neighbours; who in their turn go the next day, while the others chasing hare and deer over the hills. There were no signs around them of the slightest attempt to cultivate the soil. Their only furniture consisted of woven baskets and earthen jars, and Pule-u-le told me that in the spring he thought they should all leave and go over the "big mountain," to get from the sight of the white man.

Highly pleased with our visit, and receiving a very earnest invitation to "call again," we left the *rancheria* and proceeded towards the camp. About

ARRIVAL OF OUR PARTY

half way from the *rancheria* a loud braying, followed by a fierce growl, attracted our attention, and in a few moments a frightened mule, closely pursued by an enormous grizzly bear, descended the hill-side within forty yards of where we stood leaning on our rifles. As the bear reached the road, Higgins, with his usual quickness and intrepidity, fired, and an unearthly yell from the now infuriated animal told with what effect. The mule in the interval had crossed the road, and was now scampering away over the plains, and Bruin, finding himself robbed of his prey, turned upon us. I levelled my rifle and gave him the contents with hearty good will, but the wounds he had received only served to exasperate the monster, who now made towards us with rapid strides. Deeming prudence the better part of valour, we ran with all convenient speed in the direction of the camp, within a hundred yards of which my foot became entangled in the underbrush, and I fell headlong upon the earth. In another instant I should have fallen a victim to old Bruin's rage, but a well-directed ball from my cornpanion's rifle entered his brain and arrested his career. The whole party now came to our assistance and soon despatched Mr. Grizzly. Dragging him to camp, we made a hearty supper from his fat ribs, and, as I had probably been the more frightened of the two, I claimed as an indemnity his skin, which protected me afterward from the damp ground many a cold night. He was a monstrous fellow, measuring nearly four feet in height, and six in length, and a stroke from his huge paw would, had he caught us, have entirely dissipated the golden dreams of Higgins and myself.

SIX MONTHS IN THE GOLD MINES

Camp Beautiful

CHAPTER III.

Yuba River—A Clean Shirt an Expensive Luxury—Yankee Pedler— The Upper and Lower Diggings—Foster's Bar—The Gold-Rocker— Gold-Digging and Gold- Washing—Return to the Embarcadero— Captain John A. Sutter—Curious Currency—Sutter's Fort—Sam. Brannan and Co.—Washing Clothes—Salmon Shooting—Green Springs— Weaver's Creek—A Teamster's Bill.

NEXT morning early, in better spirits than we had enjoyed for a week previously, we started for Yuba River. About a mile from the camping-place we struck into the mountains, the same range at whose base we had been before travelling, and which are a portion of the Sierra Nevada. The hills here were steep and rugged, but covered with a magnificent growth of oak and red-wood. As we reached the summit of a lofty hill, the Yuba River broke upon our view, winding like a silver thread beneath us its banks dotted with white tents, and fringed with trees and shrubbery.

We had at last reached the "mines," although a very different portion of them than that for which we started. We turned out our tired horses, and immediately set forth on an exploring expedition. As my clothing was all dirty and wet, I concluded to indulge in the luxury of a new shirt, and going down to the river found a shrewd Yankee in a tent surrounded by a party of naked Indians, and exposing for sale jerked beef at a dollar a pound, flour at a dollar and a half do., and for a coarse striped shirt which I picked up with the intention of purchasing, he coolly asked me the moderate price of sixteen dollars! I looked at my dirty shirt, then at the clean new one I held in my hand, and finally at my little gold bag, not yet replenished by digging, and concluded to postpone my purchase until I had struck my pick and crowbar into the bowels of the earth, and extracted there from at least a sufficiency to purchase a shirt. The diggings on Yuba River had at that time been discovered only about three months, and were confined entirely to the "bars," as they are called, extending nearly a mile each way from where the road strikes the river, on both its banks. The principal diggings were then called the "upper" and the "lower diggings," each about half a mile above and below the road. We started for the upper diggings to "see the elephant," and winding through the hills, for it was impossible to travel all the way on the river's bank, struck the principal bar then wrought on the river. This has since been called Foster's Bar, after an American who was then keeping a store there, and who had a claim on a large portion of the bar. Upon reaching the bar, a curious scene presented itself. About one hundred men, in miner's costume, were at work, performing the various portions of the labour necessary in digging the earth and working a rocking machine The apparatus then used upon the Yuba River, and which has always been the favourite assistant of the gold-digger, was the common rocker or cradle, constructed in the simplest manner. It consists of nothing more than a wooden box or hollowed log, two sides and one end of which are closed, while the other end is left open. At the end which is closed and called the "mouth" of the machine, a sieve, usually made of a plate of sheet iron, or a piece of raw hide, perforated with holes about half an inch in diameter is rested upon the sides. A number of "bars" or "rifflers," which are little pieces of board from one to two inches in height, are nailed to the bottom, and extend laterally across it. Of these, there are three or four in the machine, and one at the "tail," as it is called, i.e. the end where the dirt is washed out. This, with a pair of rockers like those of a child's cradle, and a handle to rock it with, complete the description of the machine, which being placed with the rockers upon two logs, and 'the "mouth" elevated at a slight angle above the tail, is ready for operation. Modified and improved as this may be, and as in fact it already has been, so long as manual labour is employed for washing gold, the "cradle" is the best agent to use for that purpose. The manner of procuring and washing the golden earth was this. The loose stones and surface earth being removed from any portion of the bar, a hole from four to six feet square was opened, and the dirt extracted therefrom was thrown upon a raw hide placed at the side of the machine. One man shovelled the dirt into the sieve, another dipped up water and threw it on, and a third rocked the "cradle." The earth, thrown upon the sieve, is washed through with the water, while the stones and gravel are retained and thrown off. The continued motion of the machine, and the constant stream of water pouring through it, washes the earth over the various bars or rifflers to the "tail," where it runs out, while the gold, being of greater specific gravity, sinks to the bottom, and is prevented from escaping by the rifflers. When a certain amount of earth has been thus washed (usually about sixty pans full are called "a washing"), the gold, mixed with a heavy black sand, which is always found mingled with gold in California, is taken out and washed in a tin pan, until nearly all the sand is washed away. It is then put into a cup or pan, and when the day's labour is

YUBA RIVER

over is dried before the fire, and the sand remaining carefully blown out. This is a simple explanation of the process of gold-washing in the placers of California. At present, however, instead of dipping and pouring on water by hand, it is usually led on by a hose or forced by a pump, thereby giving a better and more constant stream, and saving the labour of one man. The excavation is continued until the solid rock is struck, or the water rushing in renders it impossible to obtain any more earth, when a new place is opened. We found the gold on the Yuba in exceedingly fine particles, and it has always been considered of a very superior quality. We inquired of the washers as to their success, and they, seeing we were "green horns," and thinking we might-possibly interfere with them, gave us either evasive answers, or in some cases told us direct lies. We understood from them that they were making about twenty dollars per day, while I afterwards learned, from the most positive testimony of two men who were at work there at the time, that one hundred dollars a man was not below the average estimate of a day's labour.

On this visit to Foster's Bar I made my first essay in gold-digging. I scraped up with my hand my tin cup full of earth, and washed it in the river. How eagerly I strained my eyes as the earth was washing out, and the bottom of the cup was coming in view! and how delighted, when, on reaching the bottom, I discerned about twenty little golden particles sparkling in the sun's rays, and worth probably about fifty cents. I wrapped them carefully in a piece of paper, and preserved them for a long time,—but, like much more gold in larger quantities, which it has since been my lot to possess, it has escaped my grasp, and where it now is Heaven only knows.
The labour on Yuba River appeared very severe, the excavations being sometimes made to a depth of twelve feet before the soil containing the gold, which was a gravelly clay, was reached. We had not brought our tools with us, intending, if our expedition in the mountains had succeeded, that one of our party should return for our remaining stock of provisions and tools. We had no facilities for constructing a machine, and no money to buy one (two hundred dollars being the price for which a mere hollowed pine log was offered us), and besides, all the bars upon which men were then engaged in labour were "claimed," a claim at that time being considered good when the claimant had cleared off the top soil from any portion of the bar. We returned to our camp, and talked over our prospects, in a quandary what to do. Little did we then dream that, in less than six months, the Yuba River,

then only explored some three miles above where we were, would be successfully wrought for forty miles above us, and that thousands would find their fortunes upon it.

We concluded to return to the *Embarcadero,* and take a new start. Accordingly, next morning we packed up and set off, leaving at work upon the river about two hundred men. Having retraced our steps, we arrived at Sutter's Fort in safety on the evening of November 30th, just in time to find the, member of our party whom we had left behind, packing all our remaining provisions and tools into a cart, ready to start for the "dry diggings" on the following morning.

The history of John A. Sutter, and his remarkable settlement on the banks of the Sacramento, has been one of interest since California first began to attract attention. Captain Sutter is by birth a Swiss, and was formerly an officer in the French army. He emigrated to the United States, became a naturalized citizen, and resided in Missouri several years. In the year 1839 he emigrated to the then wilderness of California, where he obtained a large grant of land, to the extent of about eleven leagues, bordering on the Sacramento River, and made a settlement directly in the heart of an Indian country, among tribes of hostile savages. For a long time he suffered continual attacks and depredations from the Indians, but finally succeeded, by kind treatment and good offices, in reducing them to subjection, and persuading them to come into his settlement, which he called New Helvetia. With their labour he built a large fort of *adobes* or sunburnt bricks, brought a party of his Indians under military discipline, and established a regular garrison. His wheat-fields were very extensive, and his cattle soon numbered five thousand, the whole labour being performed by Indians. These he paid with a species of money made of tin, which was stamped with dots, indicating the number of days labour for which each one was given; and they were returned to him in exchange for cotton cloth, at a dollar a yard, and trinkets and sweetmeats at corresponding prices. The discovery of the gold mines of California has, however, added more to Sutter's fame than did his bold settlement in the wilderness. This has introduced him to the world almost as a man of gold, and connected his name for ever with the most prized metal upon earth. He is quite "a gentleman of the old school," his manners being very cordial and prepossessing.

Sutter's Fort is a large parallelogram, of *adobe* walls, five hundred feet long by one hundred and fifty broad. Port-holes are bored through the walls, and at its corners are bastions, on which cannon are mounted. But when I arrived there its hostile appearance was entirely forgotten in the busy scenes of trade which it exhibited. The interior of the fort, which had been used by Sutter for granaries and storehouses, was rented to merchants, the whole at the annual sum of sixty thousand dollars, and was converted into stores, where every description of goods was to be purchased at gold-mine prices. Flour was selling at $60 per barrel, pork at $150 per barrel, sugar at 25 cents per pound, and clothing at the most enormous and unreasonable rates. The principal trading establishment at this time was that of Samuel Brannan & Co. Mr. Brannan informed me, that since 'the discovery of the mines, over seventy-five thousand dollars in gold dust had been received by them. Sutter's Fort is in latitude 35º 33 ' 45" N., and longitude 121º 40' 05" W.

With all our worldly gear packed in an ox-wagon, we left Sutter's Fort on the morning of the 1st of December, and travelling about seven miles on the road, encamped in a beautiful grove of evergreen oak, to give the cattle an opportunity to lay in a sufficient supply of grass and acorns, preparatory to a long march. As we were to remain here during the day, we improved the opportunity by taking our dirty clothing, of which by that time we had accumulated a considerable quantity, down to the banks of the American Fork, distant about one mile from camp, for the purpose of washing.. While we were employed in this laborious but useful occupation, Higgins called my attention to the salmon which were working up the river over a little rapid opposite us. Some sport suggested itself; and more anxious for this than labour, we dropped our half-washed shirts, and started back to camp for our rifles, which we soon procured, and brought down to the river. In making their way over the bar, the backs of the salmon were exposed some two inches above water; and the instant one appeared, a well-directed rifle-ball perforated his spine. The result was, that before dark Higgins and myself carried into camp thirty-five splendid salmon, procured by this novel mode of sport. We luxuriated on them, and gave what we could not eat for supper and breakfast to some lazy Indians, who had been employed the whole day in spearing some half dozen each. There is every probability that the salmon fishery will yet prove a highly lucrative business in California.

Next morning we packed up and made a fresh start. That night we encamped at the "Green Springs," about twenty-five miles distant from Sutter's Fort. These springs are directly upon the road, and bubble up from a muddy black loam, while around them is the greenest verdure,— the surrounding plain being dotted with beautiful groves and magnificent flowers. Their waters are delicious.

As the ox-team was a slow traveller, and quarters were to be looked for in our new winter home, on the next morning Higgins and myself were appointed a deputation to mount two horses we had brought with us and proceed post-haste to the "dry diggings." We started at 10 a.m. and travelled through some beautiful valleys and over lofty hills. As we reached the summit of a high ridge, we paused by common consent to gaze upon the landscape and breathe the delicious air. The broad and fertile valleys of the Sacramento and San Joaquin lay stretched at our feet like a highly coloured map. The noble rivers which lend their names to these rich valleys were plainly visible, winding like silver threads through dark lines of timber fringing their banks; now plunging amid dense forests, and now coming in view sparkling and bright as the riches they contain; the intermediate plains, here parched and browned with the sun's fierce rays; there brilliant with all the hues of the rainbow, and dotted with the autumnal flowers and open groves of evergreen oak. Herds of elk, black-tailed deer, and antelope browsed near the mountain sides, on the summit of which the eagle builds his eyry. The surrounding atmosphere, fragrant with delightful odours, was so pure and transparent as to render objects visible at a great distance, and so elastic and bracing as to create a perceptible effect on our feelings. Far in the distance the massive peak of Shasta reared its snow-capped head, from amid a dense forest, fourteen thousand feet into the sky. We arrived at what was then called Weaver's Creek, about dusk. About a dozen log houses, rudely thrown together and plastered with mud, constituted the little town which was to be our winter home, and where we were to be initiated into the mysteries, pleasures, and sufferings of a gold-digger's life. A pretty little stream, coursing through lofty oak and pine-covered hills, and on whose left bank the settlement had been made, was the river that had borne down the riches which we hoped to appropriate to our private uses. It was a beautiful afternoon when we reached it. The sun was just declining, and, resting upon the crest of the distant Sierra Nevada, seemed to cover it with a golden snow. The miners were returning to their log huts with their implements of labour slung over their shoulders, and their tin pans containing the precious metal in their hands. We learned that the "dry diggings" for which we had started, were three miles further into the mountains, that there was a great scarcity of water, and that but very little could be accomplished before the commencement of the rainy reason.

YUBA RIVER

Finding some old friends here, who generously offered us a "chance" upon the mud floor of their log cabin, we remained with them for the night, and stretching our blankets upon the floor and lighting our pipes, were soon engaged in an interesting conversation on the all-absorbing topic.

Next morning our party arrived with the team, and from the representations of our friends, we concluded to remain at Weaver's Creek, and pitched our tent on the banks of the stream. Our teamster's bill was something of an item to men who were not as yet accustomed to "gold-mine prices." We paid three hundred dollars for the transportation, about fifty miles, of three barrels of flour, one of pork, and about two hundred pounds of small stores, being at the rate of thirty dollars per cwt. This was the regular price charged by teamsters at that time, and of course there was no alternative but to pay, which we did, although it exhausted the last dollar belonging to our party. But there, before us, on the banks of that pretty stream and in the neighbouring gorges, lay the treasures that were to replenish our pockets, and the sigh for its departure was changed by this thought into a hope that our fondest wishes might be realized in our new and exciting occupation.

YUBA RIVER

CHAPTER IV

Our Log Cabin—Pi-pita-tua—Increase of our Party—The Dry Diggings of Weaver's Creek—The "Pockets" and "Nests"—Theory of the Gold Region—My First Day's Labour in the Placer—Extravagant Reports from the Middle Fork—Start for Culoma — Approach of the Rainy Season—The "Devil's Punch-Bowl,"

THE day after our arrival, in anticipation of the immediate commencement of the rainy season (a time dreaded by strangers in all California, and particularly in the northern region), we determined to build a log house, and were about to commence operations, when we received an offer for the sale of one. We examined it, and found a little box of unhewn logs, about twenty feet long by ten wide, which was offered us at the moderate price of five hundred dollars. The terms, however, were accommodating, being ten days credit for the whole amount. With the reasonable expectation that we could pay for our house by gold-digging in a less time than it would require to build one, we purchased it, and ere nightfall were duly installed in the premises.

Our party now consisted of ten, viz.: Higgins and a Marquesas Islander he had picked up somewhere, and who had changed his heathenish appellation of *Pi-pita-tua* to the more Christian and civilized name of "Bob;" five of our disbanded volunteers; a man by the name of Russell, the same of whom Dana speaks in his "Two Years before the Mast," and who had persuaded us to allow him to join us; the captain of the little launch "Ann," who had determined to leave the sea to try his fortune at gold-hunting, and myself. We were a queer-looking party. I had thrown aside all the little ornament's of dress, and made my best bow before the gold-digging public in red flannel and corduroy. Bob was the only member of the concern who retained what he had always in his own land considered his peculiar ornament. Right glad would he have been to rid himself of it now, poor fellow, but it was too indelibly stamped to allow of removal. It was a broad piece of blue tattooing that covered his eye on one side, and the whole cheek on the other, and gave him the appearance of a man looking from behind a blue screen. Our partnership did not extend to a community of labour in gold-digging, but only to a sharing of the expenses, trials, and labours of our

SIX MONTHS IN THE GOLD MINES

winter life.

The "dry diggings" of Weaver's Creek being a fair specimen of dry diggings in all parts of the mining region, a description of them will give the reader a general idea of the various diggings of the same kind in California. They are called "dry" in contradistinction to the "wet" diggings, or those lying directly on the banks of streams, and where all the gold is procured by washing. As I before said, the stream coursed between lofty tree-clad hills, broken on both sides of the river into little ravines or gorges. In these ravines most of the gold was found. The loose stones and top earth being thrown off, the gravelly clay that followed it was usually laid aside for washing, and the digging continued until the bottom rock of the ravine was reached, commonly at a depth of from one to six feet. The surface of this rock was carefully cleared off, and usually found to contain little crevices and holes, the latter in miner's parlance called "pockets," and in which the gold was found concealed, sparkling like the treasures in the cave of Monte Cristo. A careful examination of the rock being made, and every little crevice and pocket being searched with a sharp pointed-knife, gold in greater or less quantities invariably made its appearance. I shall never forget the delight with which I first struck and worked out a crevice. It was the second day after our installation in our little log hut; the first having been employed in what is called "prospecting" or searching for the most favourable place at which to commence operations. I had slung pick, shovel, and bar upon my shoulder, and trudged merrily away to a ravine about a mile from our house. Pick, shovel, and bar did their duty, and I soon had a large rock in view. Getting down into the excavation I had made, and seating myself upon the rock, I commenced a careful search for a crevice, and at last found one extending longitudinally along the rock. It appeared to be filled with a hard, bluish clay and gravel, which I took out with my knife, and there at the bottom, strewn along the whole length of the rock, was bright, yellow gold, in little pieces about the size and shape of a grain of barley. Eureka! Oh how my heart beat! I sat still and looked at it some minutes before I touched it, greedily drinking in the pleasure of gazing upon gold that was in my very grasp, and feeling a sort of independent bravado in allowing it to remain there. When my eyes were sufficiently feasted, I scooped it out with the point of my knife and an iron spoon, and placing it in my pan, ran home with it very much delighted. I weighed it, and found that my first day's labour in the mines had made me thirty-one dollars richer than I was in the morning.

OUR LOG CABIN

The gold, which, by some great volcanic eruption, has been scattered upon the soil over an extensive territory, by the continual rains of the winter season has been sunk into the hills, until it has reached either hard clay which it cannot penetrate, or a rock on which it rests. The gold in the hills, by the continual rains, has been washing lower and lower, until it has reached the ravines. It has washed down the ravines until it has there reached the rock, and thence, it has washed along the bed of the ravines until it has found some little crevice in which it rests, where the water can carry it no farther. Here it gathers, and thus are formed the "pockets" and "nests" of gold, one of which presents such a glowing golden sight to the eye of the miner, and such a field for his imagination to revel in. How often, when I have struck one of these have I fondly wished that it might reach to the centre of the earth, and be filled as it was at its mouth with pure, bright, yellow gold.

Our party's first day's labour produced one hundred and fifty dollars, I having been the most successful of all. But we were satisfied, although our experience had not fulfilled the golden stories we had heard previous to our reaching the *placers*. Finding the average amount of gold dug on Weaver's Creek at that time to be about an ounce per day to a man, we were content so long as we could keep pace with our neighbours. There is a spirit of emulation among miners which prevents them from being ever satisfied with success whilst others around them are more successful. We continued our labours for a week, and found, at the end of that time, our whole party had dug out more than a thousand dollars; and after paying for our house, and settling between ourselves our little private expenses, we were again on a clear track, unencumbered by debt, and in the heart of a region where treasures of unknown wealth were lying hidden in the earth on which we daily trod.

About this time, the most extravagant reports reached us from the Middle Fork, distant in a northerly direction about thirty miles from Weaver's Creek. Parties who had been there described the river as being lined with gold of the finest quality. One and two hundred dollars was not considered a great day's labour, and now was the time to take advantage of it, while in its pristine richness: The news was too blooming for me to withstand. I threw down my pickaxe, and leaving a half-wrought crevice for some other digger to work out, I packed up and held myself in readiness to proceed by the earliest opportunity, and with the first party ready to go for the Middle Fork. An opportunity soon offered itself, as a party of three who had already been there and returned, were about proceeding thither again.

SIX MONTHS IN THE GOLD MINES

We considered it a great act of generosity on their part to allow us to accompany them on their second trip, as during their first exploration on the river they had found a place where no white man had ever before trod, and where gold was said to exist in large pockets and huge bulky masses. One of my companions and myself determined to go, and if successful inform our whole party, who were then to follow.

It was now near the middle of December, and the dreaded rainy season we knew must soon commence. Occasional black clouds dimming the clearness of that mountain sky gave us warning of it; but strong in health, and stronger still in hope and determination, we heeded no warning; put our instruments of labour on the backs of two sorry-looking mules, and shouldering our rifles started away from Weaver's Creek on a fine afternoon, the clear sunshine and cooling autumn breeze playing through the lofty oak and cypress trees, giving us new vigour and new hope.

Our road for the first three miles lay across a lofty hill, which formed the dividing line (although that hill was anything but an "imaginary point extended") between our little community at Weaver's Creek and the "Dry Diggings" *par excellence* of that vicinity. On descending the hill, we found the dry diggings in a pretty little valley surrounded by hills, and forming a town of about fifty log houses. Very little was doing there, however, at that time, as the gold was so intermixed with a clayey soil, that water was necessary to separate it, and the miners were patiently waiting for the rainy season to set in. Many had thrown up huge mountain-like piles of earth, and making thereby a large excavation intended, when the rain came, to catch the water in which the golden earth was to be washed. I will give a history of the discovery and progress of these "diggings" in another part of the volume.

Passing to the northward of the Dry Diggings, we encamped at dusk in a little oak grove about three miles from Sutter's Mill, killed a deer, ate a hearty supper, spread our blankets on the ground, and slept quietly and peacefully beneath a star-studded and cloudless heaven. Next morning we went into Culoma, the Indian name for the territory around Sutter's Mill, and here we were to purchase our provisions previous to going to the river. Three stores only, at that time, disputed the trade at what is now the great centre of the northern mining region; and where now are busy streets, and long rows of tents and houses, was a beautiful hollow, which, in our romantic version, we named as we were entering it, "The Devil's Punch-Bowl." Surrounded on all sides by lofty mountains, its ingress and egress guarded by an ascent and descent through narrow passes, it seemed like a huge bowl which some lofty spirit might seize, and placing it to his lips, quaff the waters of the golden stream that circled through it. Here it was that gold was first discovered in California; this was the locality where was commenced a new era, and where a new page was opened in the history of mankind; and it is proper that I should turn out my mules to browse on the sunny hill-side shrubbery, while I stop to tell how, from this remote corner of the globe, a secret was revealed to the eyes of a wondering world.

"Dry Diggings"

CHAPTER V

Sutter's Mill—Discovery of the Placers—Marshall and Bennett-Great Excitement- Desertion of the *Pueblos,* and general Rush for the Mines—Gold Mine Prices—Descent into a Canon—Banks of the Middle Fork—Pan Washing—Good Luck—Our Camp—Terrific Rain Storm—Sudden Rise of the River.

DURING the month of January, 1848, two men, named Marshall and Bennett, were engaged in the erection of a saw-mill located by John A. Sutter on the South Fork of the American River, at a point, where oak, pine, cypress, and cedar trees covered the surrounding hills, and where Indian labour was to be procured at a mere nominal price. These were the motives that prompted Sutter to establish a mill and trading post in this, then unknown, region. Little did he imagine or foresee that, in the hands of an overruling Providence, he was to be the instrument to disclose to mankind riches of which the most sanguine daydreamer never dreamt, and open caves in which the wonderful lamp of Aladdin would have been dimmed by the surrounding brightness.

One morning Marshall, while examining the tail-race of the mill, discovered, much to his astonishment, some small shining particles in the sand at the bottom of the race, which upon examination he became satisfied were gold. Not content, however, with his own investigations, some specimens which were found throughout the whole race were sent to San Francisco by Bennett, where an assayer removed all doubt of their nature and purity. The discovery was kept a profound secret while Bennett proceeded to Monterey and tried to obtain a grant of the land on which the gold had been found from Colonel Mason, then Governor of the Territory. Colonel Mason informed him, however, that he had no authority to make any such conveyance, and Bennett returned to San Francisco, where he exhibited his specimens to Sam Brannan, Mr. Hastings, and several others. A number of persons immediately visited the spot, and satisfied their curiosity. Captain Sutter himself came to San Francisco, and confirmed the statements of Bennett, and about the 1st of April, the story became public property. Of course, the news spread like wild fire, and in less than one week after the news reached Monterey, one thousand people were on their way to the gold region. The more staid and sensible citizens affected to view it as an illusion, and cautioned the people against the fearful reaction that would inevitably ensue. Yet many a man who one day boldly pronounced the discovery a humbug, and the gold-hunters little better than maniacs, was seen on the morrow stealthily wending his way, with a tin pan and shovel concealed beneath his cloak or *serape,* to a launch about proceeding up the golden Sacramento. Before the middle of July, the whole lower country was depopulated. Rancheros left their herds to revel in delightful liberty upon the hills of their ranchos; merchants closed their stores, lawyers left their clients, doctors their patients, soldiers took "French leave." Colonel Mason, then Governor of California, was himself seized with the "mania," and taking his adjutant and an escort, started for the mines, "in order to be better able to make a report to the Government." The alcalde of San Francisco stopped the wheels of justice, and went also. Every idler in the country, who could purchase, beg, or steal, a horse, was off, and ere the first of August the principal towns were entirely deserted.

In San Francisco, the very headquarters of all the business in California, there were, at this time, but seven male inhabitants, and but one store open. In the mean time the most extravagant stories were in circulation. Hundreds and sometimes even thousands of dollars were spoken of as the reward of a day's labour. Indians were said to pay readily a hundred dollars for a blanket, sixteen for a bottle of grog, and everything else in proportion. In the mean time, new discoveries had been made at Mormon Island, as far north as the Yuba River, and as far south as the Stanislaus; and the mining population had swelled to about three thousand. The stories that had been put in circulation in regard to the richness of the *placers* were in the main true. A few months after their discovery I saw men, in whom I placed the utmost confidence, who assured me that for days in succession they had dug from the bowels of the earth over five hundred dollars a day.

But I have digressed in my narrative, and must now return to Culoma. We purchased from one of the stores two hundred pounds of flour, for which we paid three hundred dollars, one hundred pounds of pork for two hundred dollars, and sugar and coffee at a dollar a pound, amounting to another hundred dollars, making in all six hundred dollars expended for about two months' provisions. We crossed the South Fork, and mounting a lofty hill overlooking the river, encamped for the night on its summit. The next day we descended the hill, and passing through a long and watered valley, struck the "divide" or ridge, which overhangs the river at a point three miles above the "Spanish Bar," at dusk. We again encamped, anxious for a long and invigorating sleep to prepare us for a descent in the morning.

The hill was so steep and entirely trackless and covered with such a thick scrubby brush, that we abandoned the idea which we had entertained of leading our mules with their packs on down to the river; and distributing the load, each one took his share of the half of it, and commenced the terrible descent into the *canon*. A jolly good fellow, named M'Gee, a brother officer of mine in the regiment, had a good-sized buck we had killed in the morning allotted as his burden, and, pioneer like, started ahead; I followed with a bag of flour, and the remainder variously burdened, brought up the rear. The hill was so steep, and so craggy, that in many places we arrived at jagged rocks where a perpendicular descent was to be made. At one of these, Mac, who was a wild, harum-scarum fellow, had found himself just upon its very verge, from a run or slide he had made above it. He was in a dangerous position, his buck slung over his shoulders, and his only hope was to precipitate the animal down the crag into a gulf that yawned below. Down went the buck, and Mac as quickly as possible followed it; he found it two or three hundred yards below us, rendered amazingly tender by its voyage. The descent was a terrible and tedious one, and when about half way down, we first discovered the river, looking like a little rivulet, winding through its rock-girdled banks. About noon, after a two hours' tiresome travel, we reached our camping-place on the narrow river bank, and, depositing our loads, again ascended for the remainder of our provisions.

The banks of the Middle Fork, on which we encamped, were rugged and rocky. Awful and mysterious mountains of huge granite boulders towered aloft with solemn grandeur, seeming piled up upon each other as though some destroying angel had stood on the summit of the lofty hills and cast promiscuously these rocks headlong down the steep.

What a wild scene was before us! A river rapidly coursing through a pile of rocks, and on each side of it hills that seemed to reach the clouds. The mountains that overlook this river are about two miles in height, and are probably as difficult of travel as any in the world.

It puzzled us greatly to find a camping-place, although we had no tent to pitch, and only wanted room to spread our blankets on a rock. I searched the river up and down for fifty yards in this laudable endeavour, and finally succeeded in finding a little triangular crevice, formed by two boulders resting against each other, into which I crept, and slept that night, with the pleasant anticipation that the rocks above might possibly give way, in which case my gold digging dreams would meet with a woeful denouement by my being crushed to atoms. No such fate overtook me, however, and the next morning I arose fresh and hearty, to commence my first day's labour on the golden banks of the Middle Fork.

We had packed on the back of one of our mules a sufficient number of boards from Culoma to construct a machine, and the morning after our arrival placed two of our party at work for this purpose, while the rest of us were to dig; and, taking our pans, crowbars, and picks, we commenced operations. Our first attempt was to search around the base of a lofty boulder, which weighed probably some twenty tons, in hopes of finding a crevice in the rock on which it rested, in which a deposit of gold might have been made; nor were we unsuccessful. Around the base of the rock was a filling up of gravel and clay, which we removed with much labour, when our eyes were gladdened with the sight of gold strewn all over its surface, and intermixed with a blackish sand. This we gathered up and washed in our pans, and ere night four of us had dug and washed twenty-six ounces of gold, being about four hundred and sixteen dollars. The process of pan-washing is the simplest mode of separating the golden particles from the earth with which it is amalgamated. A common-sized tin pan is filled with the soil containing the gold. This is taken to the nearest water and sunk until the water overspreads the surface of the pan. The earth is then thoroughly mixed with water and the stones taken out with the hand. A half rotary motion is given to the pan with both hands; and, as it is filled, it is lifted from the water, and the loose light dirt which rises to the surface washed out, until the bottom of the pan is nearly reached. The gold being heavier than the earth, sinks by its own weight to the bottom, and is there found at the close of the washing, mixed with a heavy black sand. This is placed in a cup or another pan till the day's labour is finished, when the whole is dried before the fire and the sand carefully blown away. The gold which we found the first day was principally procured by washing, although two pieces, one weighing thirteen and the other seventeen dollars, were taken from a little pocket on the rock. We returned to camp exceedingly elated with our first attempt; and gathering some green branches of trees built a fire, cooked some venison, crawled into our holes and went to sleep.

The next day, our machine being ready, we looked for a place to work it, and soon found a little beach, which extended back some five or six yards before it reached the rocks. The upper soil was a light black sand, on the surface of which we could see the particles of gold shining, and could in fact gather them up with our fingers. In digging below this, we struck a red, stony gravel that appeared perfectly alive with gold, shining and pure. We threw off the top earth and commenced our washings with the gravel, which proved so rich, that, excited by curiosity, we weighed the gold extracted from the first washing of fifty pansful of earth, and found seventy-five dollars, or nearly five ounces of gold to be the result. We made six washings during the day, and placed in our common purse that night a little over two pounds,—about four hundred dollars worth of gold dust.

Our camp was merry that night. Seated on the surface of a huge rock, we cooked and ate our venison, drank our coffee, and revelled in the idea that we had stolen away from the peopled world, and were living in an obscure corner, unseen by its inhabitants, with no living being within many miles of us, and in a spot where gold was almost as plentiful as the pebble stones that covered it.

After working three days with the machine, the earth we had been washing began to give out, and it became necessary for us to look for a new place: accordingly on the fourth morning, we commenced "prospecting." Three of us started down, and three up the river. I sauntered on ahead of the party on the lower expedition until, about three hundred yards from camp, I found a pile of rocks that I thought afforded a reasonable "prospect." I started down to the river bank, and seated myself at the foot of a vast rock to look around me. I observed above me, and running in a direct course down the rocky bank, large crevice, which I carefully searched as high up as I could reach, but found only a very small quantity of gold. Being disappointed in this, I determined to trace the crevice to its outlet, confident that there a deposit of gold must have been made. I traced the crevice down nearly to the edge of the water, where it terminated in a large hole or pocket, on the face of a rock which was filled with closely packed gravel. With a knife and spoon I dug this at, and till when near the bottom of the pocket, I found the earth which I brought up in my spoon contained gold, and the last spoonful I took from the pocket was nearly pure gold in little lumpy pieces. I gathered up all the loose gold, when I reached the stony bottom of the pocket, which appeared to be of pure gold, but upon probing it, I found it to be only a thin covering which by its own weight and the pressure above it, had spread and attached itself to the rock. Crossing the river, I continued my search, and, after digging some time, struck upon a hard, reddish clay, a few feet from the surface. After two hours' work, I succeeded in finding a "pocket" out of which I extracted three lumps of pure gold, and one small piece mixed with oxydized quartz. Elated with my good luck, I returned to camp, and weighing the gold, found the first lot amounted to twelve and a half ounces, or two hundred dollars, and the four lumps last found, to weigh sixteen and three quarter ounces. The largest pieces weighed no less than seven ounces troy. My success this day was, of course, entirely the result of accident; but another of the party had also found a pocket containing about two hundred and seventy dollars, and a place which promised a rich harvest for our machine.

The gold thus found in pockets and crevices upon the river banks, is washed from the hills above them. In searching for the course of the metal, I have found small quantities by digging on the hilltops, and am fully persuaded that the gold is washed by the rains, until seeking, as it always does, a permanent bottom, it rests in any pocket or crevice that can prevent it from being washed further or falls into a stream running at the base of the hills, to find a resting-place in its bed, or be again deposited on its banks. If this theory be true, the beds of the rivers whose banks contain gold must be very rich in the precious metal, and recent labours in damming and turning the courses of certain portions of them, have so proved. The richest deposits of gold upon the rivers are found on what are called the "bars." These bars are places where there is an extension of the bank into the river, and round which the stream winds, leaving, of course, a greater amount of surface than there is upon the bank generally. They are covered with large rocks deeply imbedded in the soil, which upon most of them is a red gravel, extending to the solid formation of rock beneath.

There are two theories upon which the superior richness of the bars can be accounted for. The first is, that the river in its annual overflows has made the deposits of gold here, and that being more level and broad than the river's banks, they retain a larger quantity of the gold thus deposited. The other, and the only one that accounts for the formation of the bars themselves, is, that where they now are, the river formerly ran; and that they were once the river's bed, but that from some natural cause, the channel has been changed and a new one made; and thus, are left dry, these large portions of the river's bed which annually receive fresh deposits of gold from it in its overflow.

SUTTER'S MILL

We were all ready to commence operations on our new place in the morning, when, on waking, we found the sky hazy, and soon after breakfast a severe rain set in. We crept into our holes and remained there through the day, hoping for a cessation of the rain before the morning, but it continued pouring in torrents. Never have I seen rain come down as it did then and there; not only the "windows" but the very floodgates "of heaven" seemed opened upon us, and through that doleful night we lay upon our blanketed rocks, listening to the solemn music of the swollen river rushing rapidly by us, and the big rain torrents Pouring upon its breast. In the morning we found that the river had risen four feet, and observing, high above our camp, the marks of the height to which it had attained during previous seasons, we judged it prudent to be looking for higher quarters. The rain continued raising the river through the second and third days, nearly three feet more, until it nearly reached our rock-couches. We talked the matter over, and determined to leave the next day, and return to our winter quarters on Weaver's Creek. We felt, of course, a profound sorrow at leaving our rich spot, after having satisfied ourselves that a few months' labour in it would make us all wealthy men,—after having succeeded, with great labour, in transporting to it two or three months' provisions, and having suffered so much by resting (if resting it could be called) our labour-wearied bones upon rocks of the most unaccommodating and inelastic character. But the dreaded rainy season we knew had commenced, and rosy health was better than the brightest gold, so we stowed away our provisions with the exception of what we supposed would be requisite for our journey homeward, and on the fourth morning after the rain commenced, took our line of march up the formidable hill.

SIX MONTHS IN THE GOLD MINES

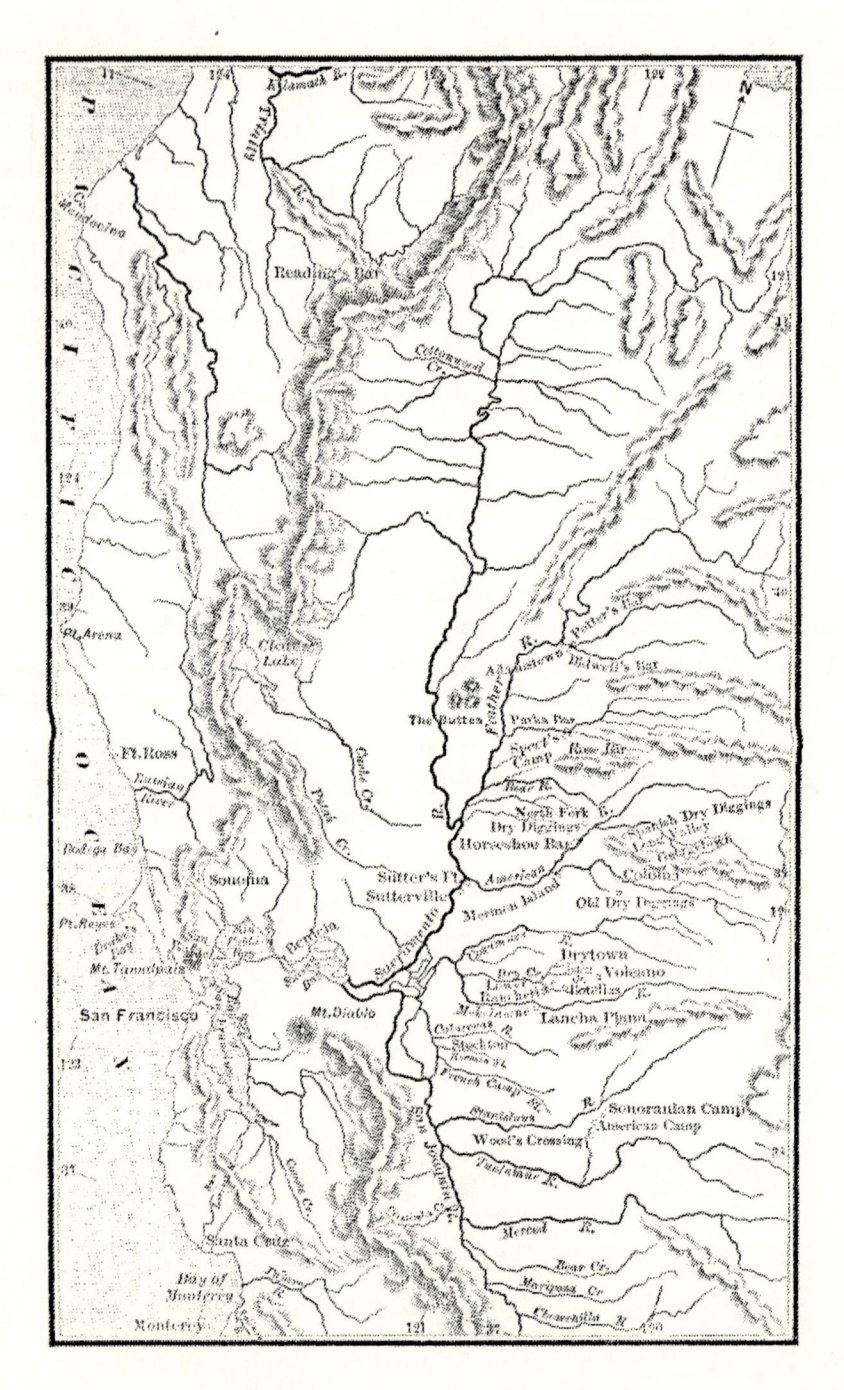

Map of the Gold Region, 1848

CHAPTER VI.

Mormon Exploration of the Middle Fork—Headquarters of the Gold-hunters—The North Fork—Smith's Bar—Damming—Great Luck of a Frenchman and his Son—Kelsey's Bar—Rise and Fall of the Rivers— Return to Weaver's Creek—Agricultural Prospects—Culoma Sawmill—An Extensive and Expensive Breakfast—"Prospecting" on the South Fork—Winter Quarters—Snow-storm—A Robbery—Summary Justice—Garcia, Bissi, and Manuel—Lynch Law—Trial for attempt to Murder—Execution of the Accused—Fine Weather—How the Gold became distributed—Volcanic Craters.

THE banks of the Middle Fork have proved richer than those of any other tributary of the Sacramento River. The fork is the central one of three streams, which rise in the Sierra Nevada, and course their way to the American Fork, a large branch of the Sacramento, into which they empty. The first exploration of the Middle Fork was made in the latter part of June, 1848, by a party of Mormons who had been at work upon the South Fork, and had left them for the hills in search of richer deposits than were found there. The first diggings were made at the Spanish Bar, which is about twelve miles in a direct line from Sutter's Mill, and has yielded at least a million of dollars. The Middle Fork has now been explored to its very source in the Sierra, but has not been found so rich above as it was below. Since my first trip there, I have travelled for thirty miles on both its banks, and never yet washed a pan of its earth without finding gold in it. When the immense tide of emigration began to pour in from the United States, the Middle Fork was the grand headquarters of the enthusiastic gold-hunters, and its banks have been torn to their very bottoms, and incalculable treasures taken from them. Within the past summer and fall, at least ten thousand people have been at work upon this river, and at the fair average of one ounce, or even ten dollars per day to a man, more than ten millions of dollars worth of gold dust have been extracted on this river alone Its banks having ceased to furnish a very large amount of gold, the river itself has in many places been diverted from its wonted course, a channel dug for it through a bar, and its bed wrought,—in many cases yielding an immense quantity of the precious metal, and in others, comparatively nothing. This is now about the only profitable labour that can be performed here, as the banks of the stream have been completely riddled; but when companies with capital and scientific mining apparatus shall commence operations here, a rich harvest will follow.

About ten miles beyond the Middle Fork, and coursing in the same direction, is another stream, the North Fork, whose banks have proved nearly equal in richness to those of the Middle Fork. Within the past spring and summer some fifteen points on this river have been dammed, the channel turned, and the bed of the river dug. In one case, a party of five dammed the river near what is now called "Smith's Bar." The time employed in damming off a space of some thirty feet was about two weeks, after which from one to two thousand dollars a day were taken out by the party, for the space of ten days,—the whole amount of gold extracted being fifteen thousand dollars. Another party above them made another dam, and in one week took out five thousand dollars. In other cases, where unfavourable points in the river were selected, little or no gold was found; and a fair average of the amount taken out, in parts of the river which were dammed, I think I can safely state at fifty dollars per day to a man.

Here is an immense field for a combination of capital and labour. As yet no scientific apparatus has been introduced, and severe manual labour alone has produced such golden results. When steam and money are united for the purpose, I doubt not that the whole waters of the North and Middle Forks will be turned from their channels, and immense canals dug through the rugged mountains to bear them off. There are placers upon the Middle Fork, where, within a space of twenty square feet, are lying undisturbed pounds of gold. This may appear startling; but facts and experience have led me to an analogical mode of reasoning, which has proved it to my own mind conclusively. A Frenchman and his boy, who were working on the Middle Fork in November, 1848, found a place in the river where they could scrape from the bottom the sands which had gathered in the crevices and pockets of the rocks. These were washed in a machine, and in four days' time the father and son had taken from the river's bed three thousand dollars, and this with nothing but a hoe and spade. Two men on Kelsey's Bar, on the Middle Fork, adopted the same process, and in two days washed from the earth, thus procured, fifty pounds of gold, amounting to nearly ten thousand dollars. The great difficulty in the way of labouring in this manner is, that there are very few places where the water is sufficiently shallow to permit it, and the river bed is so rocky, and the current so strong, that it is only in places where

MORMON EXPLORATION OF MIDDLE FORK

it becomes a pool of still water that the soil can be taken from its bottom. The width of the Middle Fork is in most places about thirty feet, and that of the North a little less. The current of both rivers is very strong, being at the rate of five or six miles an hour. The beds of these rivers are composed of huge rocks, tumbled together as they are upon the banks; and it is in the crevices and pockets of these rocks that the gold has secreted itself. Where the stream is narrow and the current strong, the probability is that there is but little gold; but where it expands, and the water becomes more quiet, the gold has settled peacefully, there to remain till the hand of some irreverent Yankee shall remove it from its hiding-place.

During the months of September, October, and November, and sometimes a part of December, the rivers are at their lowest ebb, when the water is from three to eight feet deep in the Middle and North Forks. In the latter part of December, or the early part of January, when the yearly rains commence, the rivers become swollen, sometimes rising eight or ten feet in the course of a week's rain. During the winter the rivers are continually rising and falling, as the rains cease or commence again. About the first of March, the snows which have fallen during the winter begin to melt on the mountains, and flow in little streams down the mountain sides. Every warm day raises the rivers perceptibly, sometimes to the extent of four feet in a single day, so that in the heat of summer they are fifteen feet higher than in the fall. The only practicable time for damming is in the fall, or early in the spring.

When I dropped the thread of this narrative, I left myself about to start up the hill on my return with the remainder of the party to Weaver's Creek. We found the journey up more toilsome than it had been before, as the soil was reduced to a pasty consistency into which we sank ankle deep at every step, and the rocks were rendered so slimy and slippery by the rain, that it was with great difficulty we could maintain our foothold when climbing over them. After a tedious three hours struggle, however, we succeeded in reaching the top, where we encamped again, and the next day travelled to the summit of the hill which overlooks Culoma. There we again encamped, and the following morning entered the settlement. The country between the mill and the Middle Fork is made up of a succession of hills, covered with oak trees, and interspersed with beautifully watered valleys. In these valleys the soil is a rich black loam, while the hills are barren, and of a red, gravelly soil. As yet no attempts at agriculture have been made in this region, but I am satisfied that the valleys would produce the common field crops in great profusion.

We reached the mill about nine o'clock in the morning, a little too late to get a breakfast at one of the stores, where sometimes the proprietor was sufficiently generous to accommodate a traveller with a meal for the moderate price of five dollars. The only resource was to lay a cloth on the storekeeper's counter, and make a breakfast on crackers, cheese, and sardines. In order not to make a rush upon the trade, we divided ourselves into three parties, each going to a different store. Mac and myself went together, and made a breakfast from the following items;—one box of sardines, one pound of sea-biscuit, one pound of butter, a half-pound of cheese, and two bottles of ale. We ate and drank with great gusto, and, when we had concluded our repast called for the bill. It was such a curiosity in the annals of a retail grocery business, that I preserved it, and here are the items. It may remind some of Falstaff's famous bill for bread and sack.

One box of sardines,	$16.00
One pound of hard bread,	2.00
One pound of butter,	6.00
A half-pound of cheese,	3.00
Two bottles of ale,	16.00
Total	$43.00

A pretty expensive breakfast, thought we! If I ever get out of these hills, and sit and sip my coffee and eat an omelet, at a mere nominal expense, in a marble palace, with a hundred waiters at my back, I shall send back a glance of memory at the breakfast I ate at Culoma sawmill.

We laid over at the mill during the day, and travelled a mile or two up and down the South Fork "prospecting." It appeared remarkable that here, where the gold was first discovered, and while hundreds and thousands were crowding to the mines, not a single man was at work upon the South Fork. But very little digging has ever been done at the mill, although I doubt not there will yet be found vast deposits of gold on the banks of the South Fork. We tried several places, and invariably found gold, but in such small quantities that we thought it would not be profitable to work there; and the day after, as the rain had ceased, we went into Weaver's Creek, with a huge load of blankets on our backs, sweating under a broiling sun.

We found our companions there, anxiously waiting for our return, and eager to listen to the glowing report we made them of our early success but disappointed almost as much as we were at the unfortunate ending of the affair. We determined to settle down quietly for the rest of the winter in our log house, and take our chance among the dry diggings. It had by this time commenced snowing; and from the first until the fifteenth of January it continued falling heavily, so that by the middle of January it was about four feet deep on a level. All labour was of course suspended, and we lay by in our log house, and amused ourselves by playing cards, reading, washing our clothing, and speculating on the future results of gold-digging. By the middle of January the snow ceased, and the rain again commenced; and in a few days, the snow having been entirely washed off the surface, we anticipated being soon able to recommence operations.

A scene occurred about this time that exhibits in a striking light, the summary manner in which "justice" is dispensed in a community where there are no legal tribunals. We received a report on the afternoon of January 20th, that five men had been arrested at the dry diggings, and were under trial for a robbery. The circumstances were these :—A Mexican gambler, named Lopez, having in his possession a large amount of money, retired to his room at night, and was surprised about midnight by five men rushing into his apartment, one of whom applied a pistol to his head, while the others barred the door and proceeded to rifle his trunk. An alarm being given, some of the citizens rushed in, and arrested the whole party. Next day they were tried by a jury chosen from among the citizens, and sentenced to receive thirty—nine lashes each, on the following morning. Never having witnessed a punishment inflicted by Lynch-law, I went over to the dry diggings on a clear Sunday morning, and on my arrival, found a large crowd collected around an oak tree, to which was lashed a man with a bared back, while another was applying a raw cowhide to his already gored flesh. A guard of a dozen men, with loaded rifles pointed at the prisoners, stood ready to fire in case of an attempt being made to escape. After the whole had been flogged, some fresh charges were preferred against three of the men— two Frenchmen, named Garcia and Bissi, and a Chileno, named Manuel. These were charged with a robbery and attempt to murder, on the Stanislaus River, during the previous fall. The unhappy men were removed to a neighbouring house, and being so weak from their punishment as to be unable to stand, were laid stretched upon the floor. As it was not possible for them to attend, they were tried in the open air, in their absence, by a crowd of some two hundred men, who had organized themselves into a jury, and appointed a *pro tempore* judge. The charges against them were well substantiated, but amounted to nothing more than an attempt at robbery and murder; no overt act being even alleged. They were known to be bad men, however, and a general sentiment seemed to prevail in the crowd that they ought to be got rid of. At the close of the trial, which lasted some thirty minutes, the Judge put to vote the question whether they had been proved guilty. A universal affirmative was the response; and then the question, "What punishment shall be inflicted?" was asked. A brutal-looking fellow in the crowd, cried out, "Hang them." The proposition was seconded, and met with almost universal approbation. I mounted a stump, and in the name of God, humanity, and law, protested against such a course of proceeding; but the crowd, by this time excited by frequent and deep potations of liquor from a neighbouring groggery, would listen to nothing contrary to their brutal desires, and even threatened to hang me if I did not immediately desist from any further remarks. Somewhat fearful that such might be my fate, and seeing the utter uselessness of further argument with them, I ceased, and prepared to witness the horrible tragedy. Thirty minutes only were allowed the unhappy victims to prepare themselves to enter on the scenes of eternity. Three ropes were procured, and attached to the limb of a tree. The prisoners were marched out, placed upon a wagon, and the ropes put round their necks. No time was given them for explanation. They vainly tried to speak, but none of them understanding English, they were obliged to employ their native tongues, which but few of those assembled understood. Vainly they called for an interpreter, for their cries were drowned by the yells of a now infuriated mob. A black handkerchief was bound around the eyes of each; their arms were pinioned, and at a given signal, without priest or prayer-book, the wagon was drawn from under them, and they were launched into eternity. Their graves were dug ready to receive them, and when life was entirely extinct, they were cut down and buried in their blankets. This was the first execution I ever witnessed. —God grant that it may be the last!

The bad weather had cleared off, and our gold-digging life was again commenced; and the little ravines that ran down from the hillsides afforded us ample field for labour. The regularity and extent with which the gold is scattered in California is remarkable. When wearied with our continual labour in the immediate vicinity of our house, we would sometimes start on a "prospecting" expedition some five or six miles distant. During all these

MORMON EXPLORATION OF MIDDLE FORK

searches I have never yet struck a pickaxe into a ravine without finding gold,—sometimes, however, in such small quantities as not to justify the expenditure of individual manual labour. Through this vast territory it is scattered everywhere, as plentifully as the rich blessings of the Providence that created it. Our labours usually yielded us sixteen dollars per day to each man throughout the whole winter.

Various have been the speculations upon the manner in which the gold became distributed in the gold-region of California. Some have supposed that, like the stones that cover the earth's surface, it was always there; and others, that it has sprung from some great fountain-head, and by a tremendous volcanic eruption been scattered over an extensive territory. With these latter I agree; and observation and experience have proved to me most conclusively the truth of this theory. The gold found in every placer in California bears the most indubitable marks of having, at some time, been in a molten state. In many parts it is closely intermixed with quartz, into which it has evidently been injected while in a state of fusion and I have myself seen many pieces of gold completely coated with a black cement that resembled the lava of a volcano. The variety of form, which the placer gold of California has assumed, is in itself sufficient evidence of the fact that it has been thrown over the surface while in a melted state. The earliest comparisons of the California gold were to pieces of molten lead dropped into water. The whole territory of the gold region bears the plainest and most distinct marks of being volcanic. The soil is of a red, brick colour, in many places entirely barren, and covered with a flinty rock or pebble, entirely parched in the summer, and during the rainy season becoming a perfect mire. The formation of the hills, the succession of gorges, the entire absence of fertility in many portions distinctly exhibit the result of a great up-heaving during past times. But there is one phenomenon in the mining region which defies all geological research founded upon any other premises than volcanic formation. Throughout the whole territory, so generally that it has become an indication of the presence of gold a white slate rock is found, and is the principal kind of rock in the mining region. This rock, instead of lying, as slate rock does in other portions of the earth, in horizontal strata, is perpendicular or nearly so; seeming to have been torn up from its very bed and left in this position. On the banks of the Middle Fork are several excavations, which can only be accounted for upon the supposition that they were at some time volcanic craters. There is one of these on the mountain side about five miles below the "Big Bar," from which, running down to the base of the mountains, is a wide gorge entirely destitute of verdure, while the earth around it is covered with shrubbery. This, I am fully convinced, was the bed of the lava stream that was thrown up from the crater; and in searching for gold at the foot of it, I found several pieces entirely covered with the black cement or lava, of which I have previously spoken. From all these evidences, I am fully satisfied that at some early date in the world's history, by some tremendous volcanic eruption, or by a succession of them, gold, which was existing in the form of ore, mixed with quartz rock, was fused and separated from its surrounding substances, and scattered through every plain, hill, and valley, over an immense territory. By its own gravity, and the continual washing of the rains, it sank into the earth until it reached a rock, or hard, impenetrable clay. It still continued washing and sliding down the hillside, until it reached the rivers or ravines, and in the former was washed along with its current until it settled in some secure place in their beds, or was deposited upon their banks; and in the latter, rested among the crevices of rocks.

CHAPTER VII.

Monotonous Life at Weaver's Creek—Dry Diggings Uncertain—Discovery of a Rich Ravine—Great Results of One Day's Labour—Invasion of my Ravine—Weber and Dalor—The Indian Mode of Trading—A Mystery—Settlement of Weaverville—Price of Gold-dust in the Winter of 1848—Gambling—Cost of Provisions—Opening of the Spring—Big Bar—Attack of the Land Scurvy—Symptoms and Treatment—Lucky Discovery—Progress of Culoma—Arrival of the First Steamer—Broadway Dandies wielding Pick and Shovel—Indian Outrages—Capture and Execution of Redskins.

OUR life at Weaver's Creek became exceedingly monotonous. There were about three hundred people then at work at this point, and whenever a new ravine was opened, everybody swarmed to it, and in a few days it was "dug out." Moreover, dry digging is exceedingly uncertain. Where it is necessary to search among the crevices of rocks to find the gold deposits, one may at times dig and delve through the whole day without striking a single deposit of gold. In this respect they are entirely different and far inferior in point of certainty to the wet diggings upon the banks of rivers. In the latter, where the gold is nearly equally distributed among the earth, a certain amount of labour will produce a certain reward; while in the former, success may not attend the operations of the gold-digger. There is a remarkable peculiarity in the gold of all dry diggings, which is, that the formation of gold in every ravine is different, so much so that one acquainted with the character of the gold in any certain region can easily tell by a glance at a piece of gold from what ravine it was extracted. This can only be accounted for on the theory, that in a narrow and deep ravine, where the water runs swiftly during the rainy season, the gold courses further over the rocks, and is more thoroughly washed, while in a shallow and wide ravine, where but little water runs, it settles upon the first rock on which it strikes, and retains its distinctive marks.

Tired of the old ravines, I started one morning into the hills, with the determination of finding a new place, where I could labour without being disturbed by the clang of picks and shovels around me. Striking in an easterly direction, I crossed a number of hills and gorges, until I found a little ravine about thirty feet in length embosomed amid low undulating hills. It attracted my attention, I know not why, and clearing off a place about a yard in length, I struck the soil which contained the gold. The earth on the top was a light black gravel, filled with pebbly stones, which apparently contained no gold. Below this was another gravel of a reddish colour, and in which the fine particles of gold were so mingled that they shone and sparkled through the whole of it. A little pool of water, which the rains had formed just below me, afforded a favourable place to test the earth, and scooping up a pan-ful, I took it down and washed it, and it turned out about two dollars. I continued digging and washing until I reached a slate rock, in the crevices of which I found many little nests or clusters of gold, some of them containing eight or ten dollars. These latter were intermixed with a heavy red clay from which the gold was almost inseparable. The gold was of the finest quality, both in size and richness, and I flattered myself that I had here at last found a quiet place, where I could labour alone and undisturbed, and appropriate to myself the entire riches of the whole ravine. When I reached and had explored the surface of the slate rock, I tried the experiment of breaking the rock itself into small pieces and washing it. This proved as rich as the red gravel, turning out two dollars to a pan-ful. The results of that day's labour were one hundred and ninety dollars worth of gold dust, and I returned to the house with a most profound secrecy resting on my countenance, and took good care not to expose to my companions the good luck I had experienced. But either my eyes betrayed me, or some prying individual had watched me, for the next morning, when busily at work in my ravine, I found myself suddenly surrounded by twenty good stout fellows, all equipped with their implements of labour. I could say or do nothing. Preemption rights are things unknown here, and the result of the matter was, that in three days the little ravine, which I had so fondly hoped would be my own property, was turned completely upside down. About ten thousand dollars worth of gold dust was extracted from it, from which I realized a little over a thousand. Merely the body of the ravine, however, was dug, and after it was entirely deserted, many a day I went to it, solitary and alone, and took from one to three ounces out of its banks. In the early discovery of the mines, ad the first working of the "dry diggings," it was supposed that the gold existed only in the beds of the ravines. But since a more philosophical idea of the cause of gold deposits has been entertained, it is found that, in many cases, depending upon the character of the soil, the banks upon each side prove richer in gold than the ravines themselves. The gold having descended from the hillsides, should it before reaching the ravine strike a rocky gravel or hard clay, will remain there instead of descending farther; and thus it happens universally, that when gold is found upon the sides or banks of a ravine, the soil is of one of these descriptions. Accident has proved this oftener than scientific reasoning. When we first reached Weaver's Creek, we found, in the very heart of the settlement, a ravine which seemed to have been completely "dug out," so much so that, by labouring in it, it would not yield five dollars a day to a man. Report said that nearly one hundred thousand dollars had been taken from it about the time of its discovery, and it was supposed there was little or none remaining. One day, however, about the first of February, an ignorant Irishman sank a hole about six feet deep on the bank, twelve feet from the bed of the ravine. He struck a hard, solid white clay, through which gold could scarcely penetrate, and by washing it, took out the first day nearly one hundred dollars worth of gold. This, of course, attracted crowds to the old ravine, and before a week had elapsed, nearly fifteen thousand dollars had been taken from the place which was supposed to be entirely worthless. Among the prizes was one piece weighing twenty-eight ounces, and valued at four hundred and forty-eight dollars; and I have no doubt that to this day the banks of many of the ravines are as rich in the pure metal as were their beds on the first discovery.

    The diggings upon Weaver's Creek were first wrought by a German, Charles M. Weber, a *ranchero* on the San Joaquin, who went thither in the early part of June. He carried with him articles of trade, and soon gathered around him a thousand Indians, who worked for him in consideration of the necessaries of life and of little trinkets that so win an Indian's heart. He was soon joined by William Dalor, a *ranchero* near Sutter's Fort, and the two, together with the labour of the Indians, soon realized at least fifty thousand dollars. By this time, individual labourers began to come in, and one of Dalor's men one morning started into the hills for newer and fresher diggings. He struck what was formerly called the "dry diggings," but which now goes by the euphonious name of "Hang-town," from the circumstance I have previously related as having occurred there.

    Indians still frequent this vicinity in considerable numbers, having acquired a taste for the luxuries of mouldy bread, putrescent codfish, and jerked beef, which form so large a portion of the stock in trade of the provision-dealers who supply the miners. I have often been amused to witness the singular manner in which they make their purchases. When the gold was first discovered, they had very little conception of its value, and would readily exchange handfuls of it for any article of food they might desire, or any old garment gaudy enough to tickle their fancy. Latterly, however, they have become more careful, and exhibit a profounder appreciation of the worth of the precious metal. When they desire to make any purchases from a dealer, they usually go in a party of ten or twelve, and range themselves in a circle, sitting on the ground, a few yards distant from the shop, and then in a certain order of precedence, known to themselves, but not laid down in the learned Selden, they proceed to the counter in rotation, and make their purchases, as follows: placing on the palm of the hand a small leaf or piece of paper, on which is perhaps a tea-spoonful of gold dust, the Indian stalks up to the dealer, and pointing first at his *dust* in hand, and then at whatever article he may desire, gives a peculiar grunt— *Ugh*!— which is understood to mean an offer; if the dealer shakes his head, the Indian retires, and returns with a little more gold dust, going through the same ceremony continually until a sufficient amount is offered, when the dealer takes it and hands over the coveted article. The only conceivable object of this mode of proceeding is that the poor creatures have been frequently plundered, and are afraid to trust themselves alone with a white man with too much gold upon their persons. Another peculiarity is, that if, for instance, they should purchase half a dozen hard biscuits for a teaspoonful of gold, and want several dozen, they will return with one tea-spoonful more, obtain six biscuits and retire, and then return again, and so on until they have obtained the desired quantity.

About the first of February, the rains and snows commenced again with four-fold vigour, and continued through the whole month with little or no interruption. Inured, however by our previous experience, and stimulated by an ambition that will carry men through dangers and difficulties which else would appal them, we continued our labours in right good earnest, and returned many a night to our log hut drenched with the rains that had been pouring on us through the day. A blazing log fire, and a pipe of tobacco, compensated us for the hardships we had endured, and we were ready, the next morning, to undergo the same for the like object. One morning, after a severe rain storm and swell of the river, I was passing up its banks, and gazing earnestly upon it, when my attention was suddenly arrested by the sight of gold lying scattered over the surface of the shore. I commenced

MONOTONOUS LIFE AT WEAVER'S CREEK

gathering it up, and soon had exhausted it. How it came there I was never able to satisfactorily determine. Some of the pieces, to the weight of two and three dollars, were lying ten feet above the edge of the river's bank, and every little stone had gathered round it a greater or less quantity. The first day I picked up about four ounces, and waited for another rain. It came that night, and the next morning I found gold there again as plentiful as it had been the day before. In addition to this, I observed, in the crevice of a rock nearly in the centre of the stream, a large deposit; and though it was cold and wintry weather, I bared my nether limbs, and waded in to get it. With my sheath-knife I tore it from the crevice in a very few minutes, and hurried home to dry myself, and learn the extent of my good fortune. I found that the gold I had taken from the river's bed weighed nearly three ounces. For several days I continued to find gold daily scattered over the surface of the bank, when, it suddenly disappeared, and I never saw more of it. How it came there was a mystery which I have never been able to fathom. It was either rained down from the clouds, thrown up by the river in its course, or was washed by the rains from the banks. The latter theory, however, I proved to be incorrect by washing several pans of earth from the bank, which turned out little or nothing; and the only plausible idea I can entertain on the subject is, that it was gold which had been washed from the ravines, carried by the river in its course, and deposited by it on the banks, although this theory very unsatisfactorily accounts for the great distance from the river's edge at which I found it. But if the latter theory be correct, what must be the richness of the bed of that river into which, for ages past, the ravines that open upon it have been pouring their treasures. As yet, no attempts have been made to dive into its bed,—and I doubt not, when capital and labour are combined for this purpose, immense profits will be realized.

The banks of the creek, which should be called "Weber's" instead of "Weaver's," are well lined with lofty, magnificent oak and pine trees, and the soil along the banks is capable of producing the common articles of agriculture in great profusion. A town, with the name of "Weaverville," has now been formed upon the direct site of the original settlement,—although there are miles of extent on the banks of the creek which are probably rich in gold, and will one day prove as great a fortune as already has the site of the present town of Weaverville.

Among the peculiarities consequent upon the extraction of gold, may be mentioned the fact, that in Weaver's Creek, during the whole winter of 1848, the price paid in silver or gold coin for gold dust was from six to eight dollars per ounce. I, myself, bought some hundred ounces of a Mexican for six dollars and a half. The only object in selling gold for coin was to procure specie for gambling purposes,—and gambling was the life of two-thirds of the residents there at that period. At the same time, communication with San Francisco and Sacramento City having been closed by the rains, provisions were enormously high. A few items will give an idea of gold-mine prices. Flour was selling at one dollar per pound, dried beef at two dollars, sugar at a dollar, coffee seventy-five cents, molasses four dollars per gallon, pork two dollars per pound, miserable New England rum at fifty cents per glass or eight dollars per bottle, and tobacco at two dollars per pound. At these prices, the trader and transporter realized a greater profit from the miner's labour than the miner himself; but provisions must be had, and no price, however great, could deter the labourer from purchasing the necessaries of life.

About the first of March, the long and severe winter broke up, and, tired of our winter quarters, our party made a division of the remaining provisions and cooking utensils, broke up housekeeping, and most of us started for the Middle Fork. Our travel was not diversified by anything new or strange, and, upon striking the river, we proceeded up it about eighteen miles above the "Spanish Bar" to a bar opposite the "Big Bar," where we pitched our camp, constructed a machine, and commenced operations.

The soil on this bar was exceedingly sandy, and the surface was covered with huge imbedded rocks, which required an immense amount of severe manual labour to remove. Below this was a red gravel, which was united with gold, the washing of which turned out about four ounces per day to each man. I was again dreaming of fortune and success, when my hopes were blasted by an attack of a terrible scourge that wrought destruction through the northern mines during the winter of 1848. I allude to the land scurvy. The exposed and unaccustomed life of two-thirds of the miners, and their entire subsistence upon salt meat, without any mixture of vegetable matter, had produced this disease, which was experienced more or less by at least one-half of the miners within my knowledge. Its symptoms and progress may not be uninteresting. It was first noticed in the "Dry Diggings," where, about the middle of February, many persons were rendered unable to walk by swellings of the lower limbs, and severe pains in them. It was at first supposed to be rheumatism, and was treated as such. But it withstood the most powerful applications used in that complaint, and was finally decided to be scurvy. So long as the circumstances which caused it continued, the disease made rapid progress. Many, who could obtain no vegetables, or vegetable acids, lingered out a miserable existence and died,—while others, fortunate enough to reach the settlements where potatoes and acids could be procured, recovered. I noticed its first attack upon myself by swelling and bleeding of the gums, which was followed by a swelling of both legs below the knee, which rendered me unable to walk; and for three weeks' I was laid up in my tent, obliged to feed upon the very articles that had caused the disease, and growing daily weaker, without any reasonable prospect of relief. There were, at that time, about eight hundred persons at work on the river, and hoping to get some medicine, I despatched one of my companions one morning, with instructions to procure me, if possible, a dose of salts, and to pay for it any price that should be asked. He returned at night with the consoling news that he had failed, having found only two persons who had brought the article with them, and they refused to sell it at any price.

Above me rose those formidable hills which I must ascend ere I could obtain relief. I believe I should have died, had not accident discovered the best remedy that could have been produced. In the second week of my illness, one of our party, in descending the hill on which he had been deer-hunting, found near its base, and strewn along the foot-track, a quantity of beans which sprouted from the ground, and were in leaf. Some one, in descending the hill with a bag of them on his back, had probably dropped them. My companion gathered a quantity and brought them into camp. I had them boiled, and lived entirely on them for several days, at the same time using a decoction of the bark of the Spruce tree. These seemed to operate magically, and in a week after commencing the use of them, I found myself able to walk,—and as soon as my strength was partially restored, I ascended the hill, and with two companions walked into Culoma, and by living principally upon a vegetable diet, which I procured by paying three dollars per pound for potatoes, in a very short time I recovered.

  I found matters very much changed at Culoma; the little settlement of three houses had grown into a large town. Buildings were being erected in all parts of it, and hundreds of tents whitened the plain. The steamer Oregon had just arrived at San Francisco on her first trip upward from Panama; and the fleet of sailing vessels loaded with passengers, attracted by the report of the gold discovery in the United States, had begun to arrive. All sorts of people, from the polished Broadway dandy, who never handled an instrument heavier than a whalebone walking-stick, to the sturdy labourer who had spent his life in wielding the pickaxe and the shovel, had come to California, and all for one common object,—to dig gold; and one class was as enthusiastic, and anticipated as good success, as the other. As there were no such accommodations as hotels at Culoma, everybody was living in tents, cooking their own provisions, and getting ready to pack up and proceed to the Middle Fork. Some of them had commenced working on the banks of the South Fork in the immediate vicinity of the mill, and could be daily seen sweating (for the weather by this time had become exceedingly warm) under a load of tools sufficient to dig a whole canal, on their way to, or coming from their places of labour. As I have before said, very little gold has been found in the vicinity of the mill,—and the gold-diggers there, at that time, were rewarded by not more than five dollars per day.

Most of them had brought with them some one of the many newfangled machines that were manufactured in the United States, after the reports of the gold discovery reached there, like the razors of Pindar, "to sell." They were of all imaginable shapes and sizes, some of them appearing most admirably adapted to the churning of butter. These were tried and found to fail, and have so far been invariably abandoned for the common rocker, which is, as I have before said, the best machine to be used in connexion with mere manual labour. Many of the new-comers were most woefully disappointed at the appearance of things, finding that gold, instead of lying scattered in "big lumps" over the earth's surface, was only to be obtained by the most severe toil.

About this time, reports were daily arriving at the settlements of outrages committed by Indians upon whites in the vicinity of the North and Middle Forks. A report which afterwards proved to be strictly correct, came to the mill, that a party of Indians had descended to the camp of five white men on the North Fork, while the latter were engaged in labour, had broken the locks of their rifles which were in their tents, and then fallen upon and cruelly beaten and murdered them. A large party, headed by John Greenwood, a son of the celebrated mountaineer, was immediately mustered at the mill, and started in pursuit of the Indians, and tracked them to a large Indian *rancheria* on Weaver's Creek. This they attacked, and after killing about twenty of them, took thirty prisoners, and marched to the mill. Here they underwent a trial, and six of them, having been proved to have been

MONOTONOUS LIFE AT WEAVER'S CREEK

connected with the party who killed the white men, were sentenced to be shot. They were taken out in the afternoon after their arrival, followed by a strong guard, and, as was anticipated, a little distance ahead being allowed them, they ran. They had no sooner started than the unerring aim of twenty mountaineers' rifles was upon them, and the next moment five of the six lay weltering in their blood. Soon after this, several expeditions were fitted out, who scoured the country in quest of Indians, until now a redskin is scarcely ever seen in the inhabited portion of the northern mining region. Their *rancherias* are deserted, the graves of their ancestors are left to be desecrated by the white man's foot-print, and they have gone,—some of them to seek a home beyond the rugged crest of the Sierra Nevada, while others have emigrated to the valley of the Tulares, and the whole race is fast becoming extinct.

After having remained some time at the mill, I returned to my old residence at Weaver's Creek. I found it deserted; the opening of the warm spring weather had drawn away the entire population, both of our settlement and the "Dry Diggings," to the richer *placers* of the golden rivers. I remained but a few days, when I proceeded to Sacramento City.

Discovery of a rich ravine

CHAPTER VIII.

Extent and Richness of the Gold Region of Upper California—Are the "Gold-washings" inexhaustible ?—A Home for the Starving Millions of Europe and the Labouring Men of America—Suicidal Policy of our Military Governors—Union of Capital, Labour, and Skill—A Word to Capitalists—Joint-stock Companies—The Gold-hearing Quartz of the Sierra—Experience of Hon. G. W. Wright—Extraordinary Results of pulverizing Quartz Rock—The Gold Mines of Georgia—Steam Engines and Stamping Machines—Growth of Sacramento and San Francisco.

THE gold region of Upper California is embraced in the country on the western slope of the Sierra Nevada, and extending over an already explored space of six hundred miles. Within the last six months, explorations have been made as far south as King's River, which flows into the Great Tulare Lake. Above this are the Stanislaus, Mokelunne, Tuolumne, and Mariposa, all tributaries of the San Joaquin, and upon all of which gold has been found, and daily the southern portion of the gold region is becoming more known. The two great streams, which with their tributaries, fence in the present gold region, are the Sacramento and San Joaquin. The most probable theory, however, in regard to the extent of the gold region, is, that it is in the whole range of mountains, extending from the Sierra Nevada, or rather the branches thereof, through Upper California, Mexico, Peru, and Chili, although it is positive that there are nowhere in the course of the range, such extensive and rich gold-washings as are found between the Sacramento and San Joaquin rivers. Many years before the discovery of gold at Sutter's Mill, a *placer* had been wrought at San Bernadino, about thirty miles southeast of the town of Santa Barbara. The gold was of the same character as that of the upper region, although found in much smaller quantities, and it is well known that for many years extensive gold *placers* have been wrought in the province of Sonora, one of the northern departments of Mexico.

Throughout this whole region there is not a stream, valley, hill, or plain, in which gold does not exist. It seems to be the natural product of the soil, and is borne like the sand along the river courses. In travelling over some three hundred miles of this territory, I have never yet struck a pick or a knife into any spot where gold would be likely to be deposited, without finding it in greater or less quantities. Until lately, it was supposed that the gold existed only in the ranges of the Sierra Nevada, and that what is called the "Coast Range," bordering the whole coast of California, was destitute of it. But experience has already proved the incorrectness of this theory. A party headed by Major P. B. Reading, some time in the spring of 1849, struck into the Coast Range of mountains, about two hundred miles north of Sacramento City, and are still labouring there very successfully, having found gold not only in quantities, but in large pieces and of the finest quality; and I doubt not that when the *placers* at the base of the Sierra Nevada shall have become partially exhausted, labour will be performed in various portions of the Coast Range with as good success as has already crowned the efforts of the diggers in the present gold region.

I do not believe, as was first supposed, that the gold-washings of northern, California are "inexhaustible." Experience has proved, in the workings of other placers, that the rich deposits of pure gold found near the surface of the earth, have been speedily displaced, and that with an immense influx of labouring population, they have totally disappeared. Thus, in Sonora, where many years ago fifteen and twenty, and even fifty dollars per day, were the rewards of labour, it is found difficult at present with the common implements to dig and wash from the soil more than from fifty cents to two dollars per day to a man. So has it been partially in the richer and more extensive placers of California. When first discovered, ere the soil was molested by the pick and the shovel, every little rock crevice, and every river bank was blooming with golden fruits, and those who first struck them, without any severe labour, extracted the deposits. As the tide of emigration began to flow into the mining region, the lucky hits upon rich deposits, of course, began to grow scarcer, until, when an immense population was scattered throughout the whole golden country, the success of the mining operations began to depend more upon the amount of labour performed than upon the good fortune to strike into an unfurrowed soil, rich in gold. When I first saw the mines, only six months after they were worked, and when not more than three thousand people were scattered over the immense territory, many ravines extending for miles along the mountains were turned completely upside down, and portions of the river's banks resembled huge canals that had been excavated. And now, when two years have elapsed, and a population of one hundred thousand, daily increasing, have expended so great an amount of manual labour, the old ravines and river banks, which

EXTENT AND RICHNESS OF THE GOLD REGION

were abandoned when there were new and unwrought placers to go to, have been wrought and re-wrought, and some of them with good success. Two years have entirely changed the character of the whole mining region at present discovered. Over this immense territory, where the smiling earth covered and concealed her vast treasures, the pick and the shovel have created canals, gorges, and pits, that resemble the labours of giants.

That the mere washings of pure gold will at some day become exhausted is not to be doubted, although for fifty years at least they will be wrought to a greater or less extent in the ravines of dry diggings that have been, in mining parlance, entirely "dug out," any man, with a mere sheath-knife and crowbar, can extract five dollars a day. The earth here has been thrown up from the body of the ravines in reaching the rock, and in other places the ground has been merely skimmed over, and many parts of the ravine left untouched; and upon the rivers banks the very earth that has been thrown aside as useless, and even that which has been once washed, will still, with careful washing in a pan, turn out from three to ten dollars per day. It is therefore evident that so long as even such wages as these can be made, men will be found to work the placers. The starving millions of Europe will find in the mountain gorges of California a home with profitable labour at their very door-sills, and the labouring-men of our own country will find it to their interest to settle among the auriferous hills. The miserably suicidal policy, which some of our military officers in California have attempted to introduce, has already proved not only its worthlessness, but the absolute impossibility of carrying it into effect. Never in the world's history was there a better opportunity for a great, free, and republican nation like ours to offer to the oppressed and down-trodden of the whole world an asylum, and a place where by honest industry, which will contribute as much to our wealth as their prosperity, they can build themselves happy homes and live like freemen.

Long after the present localities, where the washing of gold is prosecuted, are entirely abandoned, goldwashing will be continued by manual labour upon the plains and hills where the gold lies at a much greater depth beneath the soil than it does in the ravines and river banks, and where of course more severe labour is required. The era which follows the present successful gold-washing operations will be one, when, by a union of capital, manual labour, and machinery, joint-stock companies will perform what individuals now do. While gold can be found lying within a few inches of the earth's surface, and the only capital required to extract it consists in the capability to purchase a pick and a shovel, there is no need of combination; but when the hills are to be torn to their very bases, the plains completely uprooted, and the streams, which flow down from the Sierra Nevada to be turned from their channels, individuals must retire from the field, and make room for combined efforts.

Never in the history of the world was there such a favourable opportunity as now presents itself in the gold region of California for a profitable investment of capital; and the following are some of the modes in which it may be applied. I have before shown, and experience and observation have demonstrated it to me, that the beds of the tributaries to the two great rivers that flow from the Sierra Nevada are richer in gold than their banks have yet proved to be. There are many points, at each one of which the river can easily be turned from its channel by a proper application of machinery. Dams are then to be erected and pumps employed in keeping the beds dry. Powerful steam machines are to be set in operation for the purpose of tearing up the rocks, and separating the gold from them. The hills and plains are also to be wrought. Shafts are to be sunk in the mountain sides, and huge excavators are to bring to the surface the golden earth, and immense machines, worked by steam power, made to wash it. The earth, which had been previously washed in the common rockers, is to be re-washed in a more scientifically constructed apparatus, and the minute particles of gold, which escape in the common mode of washing, and which are invisible to the naked eye, are to be separated by a chemical process.

As yet no actual mining operations have been commenced in the gold region of California, for the two reasons, that they require a combination of labour and capital, and that the gold-washings have thus far proved so profitable as to make them the most desirable. But there is a greater field for actual mining operations in California than was ever presented in the richest districts of Peru or Mexico. The gold-washings, which have thus far enriched thousands, are but the scum that has been washed from the beds of the ore. I would not wish to say one word to increase the gold mania, which has gone out from California, and has attracted from the whole world thousands upon thousands of men who were not at all fitted to endure the hardships consequent upon a life in her mountainous regions, or the severe labour which was necessary to extract gold from the earth. It is to be hoped that this mania, however, has now given way to the "sober second thought," and that men have learned to listen to facts, and take the means to profit by them in the most proper manner. I should not consider myself as acting in accordance with duty, were I to assume the responsibility of publishing to the world an account of the gold mines of California, did I not, like the witness upon the stand, "tell the truth, the whole truth and nothing but the truth."

Throughout the range on the western slope of the Sierra Nevada, and in every little hill that branches from it, runs a formation of quartz rock, found sometimes at a few feet below the earth's surface, and sometimes rising above it in huge solid masses. This rock throughout the whole mining region has been proved by actual experiment to be richly impregnated with gold. Some of it exhibits the gold to the naked eye, while in other cases a powerful microscope is requisite to discern the minute particles that run in little veins through it. Experiments have been made in the working of this rock, which establish beyond a doubt its great richness, Hon. George W. Wright, one of the present representatives elected to Congress from California, has employed nearly the whole of the past summer in exploring the gold region, with a view of ascertaining the richness and extent of the quartz rock, and his experiments have proved so wonderful, as almost to challenge credulity even among those who have seen the progress of the mining operations in California from their commencement to the present period.

In pulverizing and extracting the gold from about one hundred pounds of this rock, Mr. Wright found, that the first four pounds yielded twelve dollars worth of gold, which was the largest yield made, while throughout the whole the smallest yield was one dollar to the pound of rock, and this in many cases where not a particle of gold could be discerned with the naked eye. Mr. Wright has now in his possession a specimen of this quartz weighing twelve pounds, which contains six hundred dollars, or more than one quarter of its weight in pure gold; and one dollar to the pound of rock is the lowest amount which he has ever extracted.

In the gold mines of Georgia, where at present nearly all the profits result from the extraction of gold from the quartz rock, a fifteen horse power machine, working twelve "stamps," will "stamp" or pulverize a thousand bushels of the rock per day. The pulverization is the most important item in the extraction of the gold, as after the rock is reduced to powder, the gold can be very easily secured either by washing or making an amalgam of quicksilver, or by a combination of both processes. Now, in Georgia, if each bushel of rock should produce twelve and a half cents, the profits would be good. If twenty-five cents, greater; and if fifty, enormous. A bushel of the quartz rock weighs about seventy-five pounds, and we thus find that instead of, as in Georgia, yielding from ten to twenty-five *cents* to the bushel, the gold rock of California at its lowest estimate will yield seventy-five *dollars,* and in many cases much more. Let us pursue this subject a little farther. If a fifteen horse power engine will pulverize a thousand bushels, or seventy-five thousand pounds per day, at the estimate which has here been made, from seventy-five to one hundred thousand dollars would be the result of a day's labour, the whole performance of which with suitable machinery would not require one hundred men. Even lowering this estimate one-half, profits are exhibited that are indeed as startling as they are true. Here is an immense field for the investment of capital throughout the world, and for the employment of a large portion of its labouring population.

The City of Sacramento had assumed a very different aspect at the time I reached it on my return from the northern mines, from that which it exhibited when I previously left it. Where the old store-ship used to be, on the banks of the Sacramento, tall-masted ships were moored, and the extensive plain on which I pitched my tent was dotted with houses. Around the fort itself, which is nearly two miles from the bank of the river, houses had begun to spring up. Building-lots which, four months previously, had sold at from fifty to two hundred dollars were now held by their owners at from one to three thousand. I looked on with astonishment at the remarkable progress, and then little thought that the ensuing six months would develop a growth, both in size and prices, which would entirely outstrip what I then witnessed.

Getting on board a launch, I spent a weary five days in sailing down the Sacramento, and arrived at San Francisco in the early part of May. What a change had occurred in six months! San Francisco, when I saw it before, was almost entirely deserted, everybody having gone to the mines. Now it was being daily recruited by the arrival of travellers across the plains, by vessels around Cape Horn, by Sandwich Islanders, Chinese, French, English, and Mexicans. The age of speculation had commenced. The building-lots which, when I landed in San Francisco, were granted by the alcaldes for the sum of fifteen dollars, and in the autumn before were worth but five hundred, had now risen in value to from three to five thousand. Hundreds and thousands of men with capital were arriving, who readily seized upon the opportunities

EXTENT AND RICHNESS OF THE GOLD REGION

for speculating. Houses were going up on the vacant lots, and the town beginning to assume an air of business. Goods of all kinds had fallen in price, owing to the arrival of fleets of loaded ships from all parts of the world, and in some eases from wilful neglect on the part of consignees. Large hotels had been erected, and life began to be rendered comfortable. Gambling in all its forms was carried on to an enormous extent, and money, as before, was almost as plentiful as the sea-sands.

SIX MONTHS IN THE GOLD MINES

"A mass meeting was held in Portmouth Square...."
February 12, 1849

CHAPTER IX.

The Mexican System of Government—Establishment of the Legislative Assembly of San Francisco—Seizure of the Town Records—Address of the Assembly recommending the Formation of a State Government—Interference of Brevet Brigadier-General Riley—Public Meeting—Organization of the State Convention—The Constitution—The Elections.

WHEN I arrived in San Francisco, the causes had already been set in operation which have worked out for California a state government; and though they sprang out of a local question, the result was a general one. The tracing of these causes may not be uninteresting to those who are looking upon California now as a full-grown state.

As the town of San Francisco began to fill up with American citizens, lovers of law and order, it was thought necessary that a better form of town government than then existed was requisite to secure the rights of person and property. Thus far the old Mexican system of *alcaldes* or chief-justices, and *ayuntamientos* or town councils, had been retained, and the people were living under a law which they did not understand; a law subject to great abuses, in the hands of those who did not themselves comprehend it; and it was determined that the system should be changed, and one which was understood be substituted. In compliance with a call signed by a large number of respectable citizens of the town, a mass meeting was held in Portsmouth Square on the afternoon of February 12th, 1849, when, after organizing in the usual form, and hearing the remarks made by several gentlemen, a series of resolutions were offered and unanimously carried, by which it was determined to form, for the government of the district of San Francisco, a legislative assembly, which should enact laws, and that three judges and other necessary officers should be elected to administer them.

On the 21st day of February, an election was held, in compliance with the above resolutions, and a legislative assembly, consisting of fifteen members, three judges, a register, and sheriff, was elected. One of the first acts of the Legislative Assembly, which only claimed authority over the district of San Francisco, was to abolish the office of alcalde, considering it not only unnecessary, but incompatible with American institutions; and in compliance with the act of the Assembly, Myron Norton, Esq., chief-magistrate, directed a note to T. M. Leavenworth, late *alcalde,* requesting him to deliver to the new government the records of the town. To this note Mr. Leavenworth made no reply, and another one of the same tenor was sent by Mr. Norton. This received the same treatment as the first. Trouble appeared to be brewing, and, as is usual in such cases, many, who had been the first to propose and aid the new movement, were found at this time most woefully wanting. A code of laws had already been established by the Assembly, and the wheels of the new local government were ready to be put in operation, when it was found very difficult to procure a quorum for business at the meetings of the Legislative Assembly, and it was decided that additional members should be added thereto. On the 11th of May, another election was held, at which a large and respectable vote was cast, and ten members of the Assembly were chosen— and, some informality having occurred at the previous election, a register, sheriff, and treasurer. Among the newly-elected members was Peter H. Burnett, now governor of the new state of California. Previous to this time, a letter had been addressed by a committee of the Assembly to General Persifer F. Smith, who was at the time principal military commander in California, to which was received a decidedly non-committal reply. But it was understood that Brevet Brigadier-General Riley, who had assumed the civil government of the territory, would support the old authorities, and, if possible, crush the Legislative Assembly.

California, and San Francisco in particular, were in a curious political state of existence. From the time of the treaty of peace with Mexico until the arrival of Generals Smith and Riley, Colonel R. B. Mason, who had, during the war, been military commander and governor of California, had continued in the exercise of his authority, and the country had been ruled by the same laws and usages as during the war, when it was actually a territory belonging to Mexico. In express contradiction of at least the intention and understanding of the government at Washington, Colonel Mason had appointed collectors, and collected revenue in the ports of California, and in all respects the military government had been continued; and now, when the people of San Francisco, in their sovereign capacity, had established a local government for their own protection, they found themselves interfered with by a military commander.

THE MEXICAN SYSTEM OF GOVERNMENT

The Legislative Assembly, however, went on, receiving, as it did, the support of the whole community. A courthouse was established, and courts organized; and Judge Norton finding that Mr. Leavenworth still made no reply to his note, after waiting a reasonable time, issued a writ of replevin, and gave it into the hands of the sheriff, who called upon Mr. Leavenworth at his office, presented it, and demanded the surrender of the town records. Mr. Leavenworth refused to deliver them, and the sheriff, calling to his assistance a number of the citizens, seized the records, and deposited them in the court-house. Mr. Leavenworth started for Monterey the same evening, to consult with General Riley upon future proceedings. In the mean time, the Legislative Assembly issued an address to the people of California, earnestly calling upon them to assemble in convention, and organize a provisional government for the territory, prior to an immediate application to Congress for admission as a state.

This was in the early part of the month of June, and was the first concerted movement coming from any authorized body to recommend the formation of a state government for California. Mr. Leavenworth returned from Monterey, and, acting in the double capacity of a "returned officer" and a bearer of despatches, brought with him two proclamations issued by Gen. Riley, which were dated, one the 3d, and the other the 4th of June, and were found posted up in several parts of the town the morning after Mr. Leavenworth's arrival. The streets of San Francisco, on the morning of the 10th of June, presented a most exciting scene. Little knots were gathered around the streets engaged in loud discussion, and crowds were collected in the vicinity of the proclamations reading them. The first was a long one, and commenced by stating that as Congress had failed to extend a government over California, it became the duty of the people to organize one; that he, (Gen. Riley) "in accordance with instructions from the *Secretary of War*," had assumed, for the present, the civil government of the territory, and that he conceived it his duty to organize the old Mexican system, and put it in active operation until such time as a constitution and laws should have been created. The document was one of the most inconsistent and contradictory nature, assuming, firstly, that the territory of California was, and must of necessity, as a conquered territory, continue to be under the laws and usages of Mexico, until Congress should

87

extend over it those of the United States; and at the same time calling upon the people to assemble and organize a government for themselves. The whole broad ground which had been taken by the Legislative Assembly of San Francisco, which was that, in the absence of a government extended over us by Congress, we had the inherent right to establish one for ourselves, although denied by Gen. Riley in the first part of his proclamation, was essentially admitted and urged in the latter portion.

The second proclamation was addressed merely to the citizens of San Francisco, in relation to the seizure of the town records by order of Judge Norton, and called upon all good citizens to assist in restoring them to the "proper authorities."

Various were the feelings excited, and as various the opinions expressed in regard to these proclamations, but a large majority of the people of San Francisco were fully decided in the idea that Gen. Riley had assumed an authority, which, even if it was "in accordance with the instructions of the Secretary of War," was one which he had no right to assume, and was in fact nothing more nor less than an unjust usurpation of power.

Trouble was again anticipated, and it was understood that, backed by Gen. Riley's proclamation, the former *alcalde,* Mr. Leavenworth, would attempt the re-seizure of the town records. A few days after the publication of this document, a writ was served upon the town Register, calling for their delivery; he refused to give them up, and when an attempt was made to seize them, a force of about fifty of the most respectable citizens, gathered at the courthouse, determined, if necessary, to resist *vi et armis.* The *alcalde's* sheriff presented his writ, and was replied to by Wm. M. Stewart, presiding judge, that the records could not be removed, and seeing that a strong party was arrayed against him, he left without making any forcible attempt to take them. Gen. Riley refused to lend the alcalde the assistance of any military force, and matters were soon progressing again as before.

On the 12th of June, a large meeting was held in Portsmouth Square, for the purpose of taking steps towards the establishment of a state government for California. The call for this meeting had been signed by a large number of respectable citizens, and was issued before Gen. Riley's proclamations were published, and could therefore have no connexion with them. This meeting was addressed by Hon. T. Butler King,

THE MEXICAN SYSTEM OF GOVERNMENT

Hon. Wm. M. Gwin, William A. Buffum, Esq., and other speakers, all of whom urged the propriety of the immediate formation of a state government for California.

In reply to the proclamations of Gen. Riley, an address was issued by the Legislative Assembly of San Francisco, written by Peter H. Burnett, the present governor of California, setting forth in a clear and succinct manner, the right of the people, in the absence of a territorial government established by Congress, to legislate for themselves, and justifying, in a masterly way, the course which had been pursued by the Legislative Assembly.

In order to avoid all difficulty and confusion, and arrive, by the shortest and most practicable mode, at the "consummation devoutly to be wished," the establishment of a state government for California, the Assembly and their supporters united cordially with the other citizens of California, and on the first day of August an election was held in accordance with the proclamation of Gen. Riley, at which were chosen the various local officers, and members of convention, to meet at Monterey, on the first of September, for the purpose of forming a constitution.

The convention met, and a more sensible and dignified body of men never assembled in any portion of the world. After six weeks severe labour, a constitution was prepared and laid before the people of California for their ratification or rejection. It was a constitution of the most radically democratic character, and most admirably adapted to the wishes and wants of the people over whom it was to be extended.

On the 18th day of November an election was held, at which the state constitution received an almost unanimous ratification, and at the same time a governor, and the necessary state officers, members of the state legislature, and two members of Congress, were chosen. The choice for governor fell upon Peter H. Burnett, Esq., one of the early emigrants to Oregon, and who there received the appointment as judge of the Supreme Court, an enterprising citizen of California, and one of the first to declare the rights of her people. John M Dougal, Esq., formerly of Kentucky, was elected lieutenant-governor, and George W. Wright, and Edward Gilbert, representatives to Congress. The first State Legislature met at the capital, the Pueblo de San Jose on the 15th of December, and elected Hon. John C. Fremont, and Wm. M. Gwin, Senators to the Congress of the United States. The action of Congress is thus alone necessary to constitute California one of the sovereign states of the American Union, and it is earnestly to be hoped that that august body will no longer trifle with the interests or the demands of so great and powerful a people. The struggles of California have been arduous, her trials severe; she has been taxed for the support of the general government, while not even a shadow of protection has been extended over her; and has been ruled by a military power against her own wishes, till her people have risen in their might and demanded that they should have a voice and a representation in the councils of the nation.

In tracing the causes which have created California a state, it will be seen that that little body of men, the Legislative Assembly of San Francisco, were the first to set the ball in motion, and I cannot refrain from giving them the credit which is their due. The proclamation of General Riley would probably not have been issued to this day, had not the body of which I have spoken taken the preliminary steps, and although General Riley deserves gratitude from the people for what he did, and as a man, is one of "nature s noblemen," I shall ever look upon his assumption of power as Civil Governor of California as unwarranted and unjust.

SIX MONTHS IN THE GOLD MINES

CHAPTER X.

Growth of San Francisco — Number of Houses erected — Prices of Real Estate — Rents Wages of Mechanics and Labourers — Gambling — Prices Current — Climate — Churches — Steamboats — Statistics of Shipping, &c., &c., &c.

WITHIN the past six months, the growth of San Francisco has been enormous. During that time, at least a thousand houses have been erected, of all sizes and forms. The hills around the town are now covered with buildings, and every spot of ground near the centre is occupied. When it is taken into consideration, that lumber during this time has never been lower than two hundred and fifty, and often as high as four hundred dollars per thousand, and carpenters' wages have been at from twelve to twenty dollars a day, it must be conceded on all hands, that the Californians are at least an enterprising people. During this time the price of real estate has risen in proportion with the growth of the town, property being now fifty per cent higher than it was six months since. A lot on Portsmouth Square, which was purchased some three years ago for fifteen dollars, and sold last May for six thousand, was purchased a few days since for forty thousand dollars! The mere ground-rent of a little piece of land of sufficient size to erect a house upon, in any of the public streets, varies from one hundred to five hundred dollars per month. Rents of houses are, of course, in proportion to the price of real estate. A common-sized lodging-room, anywhere near the centre of the town, rents for one hundred dollars per month; an office on a lower floor, from two hundred to five hundred. The "Parker House," a hotel upon the Square, is leased for two hundred thousand dollars per annum, and under-leased in small portions, at a profit of fifty thousand more. In the "El Dorado," a large building next to the Parker House, a single room on the lower floor is rented for gambling purposes, for one hundred and eighty dollars a day, or five thousand four hundred dollars a month—nearly sixty-five thousand dollars per annum. Most of the large rooms in the hotels are rented to gamblers, each table where a game is played paying thirty dollars a day. A man who erects a house in San Francisco usually intends that the rent should cover all expenses of the building in three or four months, and in this he generally succeeds. Mechanics command enormous wages. Carpenters are now getting from twelve to twenty dollars a day, and tin-smiths, bricklayers, paper-hangers, and others employed in the construction of buildings, the same; while common day-labourers engaged in discharging vessels, digging cellars, &c., command eight dollars a day for their services. Board varies from sixteen to forty dollars per week, and washing costs eight dollars per dozen. A bewildered stranger, in search of a night's lodging, may procure one by sleeping upon a narrow shelf called a "bunk," at the moderate charge of two dollars, and get his breakfast at an eating-house in the morning for a dollar and a half. Many of the common articles of trade, such as clothing, can be obtained here almost at New York prices.

San Francisco possesses one of the most capacious and magnificent harbours in the world; one in which the navies of all the maritime powers could ride at anchor in perfect safety. From its entrance to its head is a distance of about twenty miles, and branching from it are two other large bays—San Pablo, and Suisun. The entrance to the harbour is guarded by lofty hills, about five thousand feet apart, and could be protected with the greatest ease. But the town of San Francisco itself is not fitted by nature as a pleasant residence. During the spring, summer, and autumn, cold northwest winds are continually blowing, sometimes with such severity as to destroy buildings, and always filling the streets with a dense cloud of dust. From December to March, during the continuance of the rainy season, the streets, which have been filled with dust in the summer, become perfect pools of mud and mire, so that in some of them it is almost impossible to travel. The climate is one of the most peculiar in the world. During the summer the weather is so cold that a fire is always needed, and the surrounding hills are dry and burned up; while in the winter, in the intermissions between the rains, the weather is delightfully warm and May-like, and the hills become clothed with a lovely verdure. Among the improvements in the town are several wharves, which have been completed within a short time past. The principal of these, the central wharf, built by a joint-stock company, extends into the harbour a distance of two hundred and ninety-two feet, and will, when completed, be twenty-one hundred feet in length, enabling vessels to lie abreast, and discharge their cargoes directly upon it. Several churches have also been erected; and there are now in the town seven, of the following denominations, viz.: Catholic, 1; Episcopalian, 2; Baptist, 1; Presbyterian, 2; Methodist, 1. There are also two public schools in operation. Some ten or

SIX MONTHS IN THE GOLD MINES

twelve steamboats are plying on the Sacramento and San Joaquin rivers, and the bay of San Francisco; so that travelling has ceased to be so disagreeable as it was when I went up the Sacramento in a little open boat. These steamboats run to Benicia, Sacramento City, Stockton, and San Jose; while several smaller ones ply up and down the Sacramento River, to and from the various little towns upon it. The passage from San Francisco to Sacramento City, a distance of one hundred and eighty miles, is performed in nine hours; the price of passage being twenty-five dollars.

The following table, kindly furnished me by the Collector of the port, exhibits the amount of tonnage in San Francisco on the 10th of November, 1849, together with the number and national character of the vessels in the harbour.

American tonnage, ... 87,494
Foreign tonnage, ... 82,823
   Total amount of tonnage, ... 120,317

No. of ships in harbour, ... 312
No. of ships arrived from April 1st, to November 10th, ... 697
   Of which there were,
      American, ... 401
      Foreign, ... 296

CHAPTER XI.

Weber—Sullivan—Stockton—Hudson—Georgetown—Sam Riper—
 The Slate Range—The "Biggest Lump" yet found in California.

THAT immense fortunes have been made in California is beyond a doubt; many of them, assuredly, have been by gold-digging and trading, the latter occupation, in some cases, proving even more profitable than the former. The man who has been most fortunate in the mines is, probably, Charles M. Weber, a German, of whom I have previously spoken, who left his rancho on the first discovery of gold, and collecting a large herd of Indians, placed them at work at various mining points, finding them in provisions, and purchasing their gold from them with blankets at a hundred dollars apiece, and every other article of trade at correspondingly enormous prices. The untutored Indian, who had spent all his life in roaming over his native hills, subsisting upon acorns and wild game, and clothed in the skins of the deer and the wolf the moment he found himself able to live sumptuously upon flour, and some of the little luxuries of life, and clothe his swarthy limbs in an elegant Mexican *serape* or Yankee blanket, was ready to part with his gold, of the value of which he had no idea, on the most accommodating terms. I have seen Indians at Culoma, 'who, till within the previous three months, had been nude as newborn babes, and had lived on roots and acorns, clothed in the most gaudy dresses, and purchasing raisins and almonds at sixteen dollars a pound.

It is said that Weber, before he gave up the digging of gold, had, by the labour and trade of the Indians, made between four and five hundred thousand dollars. He then purchased the ground on which the flourishing town of Stockton now stands, laid it out in building lots, and is now probably worth over half a million of dollars, and his present trade and sale of lots will, without doubt, double this amount in one year.

John Sullivan, an Irishman, who, when I first arrived at San Francisco, was driving an ox-team, some time in the summer of 1848, discovered a *canon* near the Stanislaus River, which proved so rich that crc the winter was over he had taken from it twenty-six thousand dollars worth of gold dust. With this he established a trading post, purchased property in San Francisco, and is now on the highroad to a large fortune. The *canon* he discovered has ever since been called Sullivan's Diggings, and has been celebrated for the "big lumps" which have been taken from, it.

A man named Stockton, who came to California in the same ship with me, and who was a private in our regiment, settled upon the Stanislaus River, in the early part of September, 1848. He was a keen, trading genius, and, striking out of the beaten track, bought a mule, and started, with a small lot of trinkets and little articles of luxury, into the mountain Indian region. Here his faculties "for driving bargains" were brought into full play, and it is said to be a fact, that he has sold several boxes of raisins to the Indians at their weight in gold! Stockton made a great deal of money; but lately, through some mismanagement in his business, has, I believe, failed, and commenced the world over again.

A young man named Hudson, from New York, I think, discovered a deep *canon* between the town of Culoma and the Middle Fork, about eleven miles distant from the former place, and six from the latter. This is a place which, in my travel to the Middle Fork and back, I have crossed four times without ever thinking of disturbing it. But in the summer of 1849, Hudson struck into it, and by digging some four feet reached the granite bed of the *canon,* on which lay immense masses of gold. In the course of six weeks he had dug some twenty thousand dollars. The gold in this *canon* is all large and of the purest quality, being generally entirely exempt from the admixture of quartz, which is usually found in large pieces. The largest piece found here, and which I had the pleasure of seeing, weighed a little over fourteen pounds clear gold, and was worth nearly two thousand eight hundred dollars. The success of every one who has worked in this *canon,* has probably been more uniform than in any other place in the whole mining region.

A boy, nineteen years of age, named John C. Davenport, from New Bedford, took out here, one day last fall, seventy-seven ounces, and the next day nearly ninety ounces of pure gold. The *canon* I have above referred to is now called Georgetown, and has become a thriving little community, there being, at present, about two thousand people digging there, who have built themselves comfortable log houses, and have settled down quietly to labour and enjoy the fruits of their toil.

A young man, named Samuel Riper, from Waterloo, New York, who, with three companions, went on to the Yuba River in June, 1849, in company with Dr. Bullard, dammed off a place about fifty miles above the river's mouth, seventy feet long by twenty-five feet wide. By severe labour, occupying the party of four nearly a fortnight, they succeeded in perfectly drying this part of the river s bed, and commenced washing the earth they found in it, consisting of a red gravel, solidly packed into the crevices of the rock. The earth turned out about three hundred dollars per day, and in less than two months the party of four divided among themselves the sum of fifteen thousand dollars! Immediately above this, two of the same party dammed a much smaller place, and in two weeks took out three thousand dollars worth of gold.

About seventy miles from the mouth of the Yuba River is a curious formation of rock called "The Slate Range;" it is upon the bank of the river, and extends along it. Above it are lofty and precipitous hills, exceedingly difficult and dangerous of descent,—but the richness of the slate rock beneath has well compensated all who have endured the toil of descending. The slate lies about four feet below the earth's surface, and between the thin strata the gold is found adhering to the rock. Over sixty thousand dollars worth of gold has been taken from this range during the past summer.

But one of the most curious circumstances in connexion with the gold mines occurred at the old "Dry Diggings," of which I have previously spoken. These were entirely deserted last spring, having been used as a mere wintering place, and abandoned when the weather admitted of travelling. As emigration rushed in, however, people again began to settle at the old working-places, and the "Dry Diggings" were soon again filled up. The houses were placed in a long valley, through which a stream ran, and as the diggings thus far had all been found in the ravines which run up into the hills,—no one ever thought of trying the valley itself, which was in fact nothing more than a ravine of a larger kind. But within the past summer this whole valley has been completely dug up, and immense quantities of gold have been taken from it. Even the ground on which the houses stood has been uprooted, and one man named Wilson took from under his own doorstep about two thousand dollars worth of gold. In another case, three Frenchmen removed the stump of an old tree which lay across the pathway on the road from the dry diggings to Culoma, commenced operations, and in one week dug nearly five thousand dollars. I might go on multiplying instances of extraordinary success in gold-digging. But so many stories of this nature are already in circulation, that I will merely add one more.

Dr. H. Van Dyke, with a company of about thirty men, went on to the North Fork in August last, and constructed a dam on that river just above its junction with the American Fork. Within the first three days after the drainage was completed, the company had taken out fifteen thousand dollars; and afterwards, for nearly a month, made from five to twelve ounces a day per man.

The largest piece of gold which has yet been found was picked up in a dry ravine near the Stanislaus River, in September, 1848. It contained a large admixture of quartz, and weighed a little over twenty-five pounds, being worth five thousand dollars. A piece weighing twenty-seven ounces and a half was found by a young man named Taylor at "Kelsey's Dry Diggings," on the South Fork, about eight miles from Culoma. I saw this piece at the Mill last spring, and it is now in the possession of Hon. Edward Gilbert, one of our representatives in Congress from California. It is a beautiful specimen, about six inches in length, the gold being inlaid in a reddish stone. This piece was found by pure good luck, having been probably thrown up from the ravine in some loose dirt, where, it was picked up by Taylor, lying directly on the surface.

CHAPTER XII.

Recapitulation—Population of the Mining Region—Average Amount of Gold Dug—Requirements of a Gold-Digger—The Best Season—In what kind of Soil is Gold Found?—Washing Machines—California a Habitable Country—The Learned Professions.

IT is proper, before closing this work, and it will probably be expected, that I should make a sort of recapitulation, and give some advice in regard to prospects and plans of proceeding in the gold mines of California. To advise is always a difficult task, and in this instance it is peculiarly so; but I will endeavour to give a fair statement of facts, and the best advice I can. The number of persons at present labouring in the various portions of the mining region is about one hundred thousand. Of these, at least one-third are Mexicans, Chilenos, Pacific Islanders, and Chinese, and the remainder Americans, English, French, and Germans; and I should divide their locations as follows: on the North, Middle, and South Forks, say twenty thousand; on the Stanislaus, Mokelumne, Tuolumne, Merced, Mariposa, and other tributaries of the San Joaquin, forty thousand; on Yuba and Feather Rivers, twenty thousand; and, scattered over the various dry diggings, twenty thousand more. During the past summer and autumn, I should estimate the average quantity of gold dug daily at eight dollars to a man; for although it is by no means uncommon for an individual to "strike a lucky place," and some days take out from a hundred to a thousand dollars, others spend whole days in search and labour, without finding more than two or three dollars a day. From my own experience in the mines I am, however, satisfied, that, during six months in the year, a stout man, with health, energy, and perseverance, can average sixteen dollars a day in almost any portion of the placers; and that, for twenty years, from three to ten dollars a day can be made by individual labour. Still, I would advise all who are in good positions at home to remain there. The labour and hardships consequent upon the life of a gold-digger are of the most severe and arduous nature. Prying and breaking up huge rocks, shovelling dirt, washing it with wet feet all day, and sleeping on the damp ground at night, with nothing above but a thin covering of canvass, or a leaky log roof, are not by any means agreeable to one who has been accustomed to the civilized life of cities.

SIX MONTHS IN THE GOLD MINES

Richelieu says, that "the pen is mightier than the sword." Many a fine, spruce young clerk coming to California with golden dreams of wealth before him has proved, to his sorrow, that the crowbar is heavier than the pen. I hesitate not to say, that the labour of gold-digging is unequalled by any other in the world in severity. It combines within itself the various arts of canal-digging, ditching, laying stone walls, ploughing, and hoeing potatoes,— and adding to this a life in the wilds of the mountains, living upon poor provisions, continually exposed either to the burning rays of the sun, or the heavy dews of night, and the occupation becomes anything but a pleasant one. But to a man endowed with a constitution to endure hardship, with hands that have been accustomed to labour, and with a heart which suffers not itself to be sorrowed with disappointment, there was never a better opportunity in the world to make a fortune, than there is at present in California. To mechanics, especially, there are great inducements; for if they do not choose to labour in the mines, with the wages which I have previously stated as being paid to them in San Francisco and the other towns of Northern California, they may, in one year, save more money than in five in any other portion of the United States.

To those who do come, I would give a few words of advice, which may be of service. Bring with you very little clothing and provisions, as they will only prove a burden. These can be purchased in San Francisco almost at New York prices. Never come without money, as gold is not to be found in the streets of San Francisco. You may be delayed several days before going to the mines, and board at from, sixteen to fifty dollars a week will soon make a large hole in a small sum of money. Arrived at San Francisco, beware of the vices prevalent there. Drinking and gaming are the principal, and in fact the only amusements of the town, and many a poor fellow, landing there with high hopes, has been fleeced and turned adrift upon society with a broken heart. Purchase no provisions in San Francisco. The expenses of transportation are so great, (freight up the river being from two to four cents per pound, and by teams to the various mining points from fifteen to fifty,) that your provisions will cost more in money and time than they would if purchased in the mines. Flour is now selling in the gold regions at about fifty cents per pound; this seems like a great price, but you will find it cheaper than to carry it with you, and will soon find that it is much easier to pay fifty cents for a pound of flour when you are making sixteen dollars a day, than it is to pay three cents when you are making but one. For the same reason that you should carry no provisions, carry but little clothing. A mere change is sufficient, and clothes can always be purchased at reasonable rates in all parts of the mines.

The best season for proceeding to the mines is about the end of the month of August. The waters which have been swollen by the melting of the snows in the summer, have then subsided, and the heat of the summer months has then given way to the cooling breezes of autumn. From that time till the middle of December, the weather is most delightful, and the opportunities for profitable labour are far better than at any other time. About the middle of December, the rainy season commences; the rivers immediately commence rising, and labour is prevented both by this and the inclemency of the weather. The life of the miner during the winter months is exceedingly unpleasant, and I would advise no one to proceed to the gold region after the month of November. The rainy season usually closes about the middle of February, but the roads are exceedingly muddy until the first of March, and from that time till July, labour can be performed to advantage in the various dry-diggings, and upon some of the rivers. By this time the hot and sickly season commences, and the waters upon the rivers are at their greatest height. The thermometer ranges from 90^0 to 120^0 in the shade at noonday, and the heavy dews of night fall upon the labourer, who has been all day at work beneath a broiling sun. This of course produces disease, and in that wild region, where the comforts and attendance that should ever surround a sick man's bed, are unknown, disease is usually followed by death. The most prevalent diseases during this time are fever and ague, and bilious fevers of the most virulent nature. But I am satisfied that, setting aside the prevalence of diseases common to all new countries, a large portion of the sickness of the summer months is caused by the exposure consequent upon the present mode of life of the miner. When the same comforts are introduced, when good houses are built, and wholesome provisions can be procured, the mining regions of California will compare favourably with Illinois, Indiana, or any of the new states in point of healthiness.

It has been a frequent inquiry in the United States, "In what kind of soil is gold found?" The answer is, that is found in no one particular kind of soil, but in every variety from the common loose black earth to the hardest clay. I have found, in the dry diggings of Weaver's Creek, pieces of gold, some of them weighing nearly a quarter of an ounce, lying in the upper black soil within two inches of the surface. It is sometimes found embedded in a hard white clay, at other times in a red, and at others in a blue clay. As a general thing, I have found that where the gold is coarse, it usually descends until it reaches one of the above-mentioned clays, while the finer particles rest upon the gravelly stratum nearer the surface, and thus fine gold is most frequently found mingled with red gravel.

In regard to bringing machines to California for the purpose of washing gold, I must caution the miner to be careful and judicious in their selection. Some of the more recent inventions are valuable, especially the "Quicksilver Gold Separator," which is constructed to operate with quicksilver in such manner as to save the fine particles of gold which in the ordinary cradles or rockers are lost. The only object of a machine of any kind is to break up and keep in motion a larger quantity of earth than a pan would hold, and at the same time prevent the gold from being lost. I saw, last spring, hundreds of huge, bulky machines, which had been brought round Cape Horn, and which would require, each one of them, a large ox-team to convey them to the mining region, lying piled upon the beach of San Francisco, destined never to fulfil the object for which they were intended, and ere this probably used for firewood, or in constructing habitations for their owners to dwell in. There are, however, some small hand machines manufactured in New York, which are really of great use to the gold-digger.

A great mistake has been made by people who have emigrated to California, or who have desired to emigrate, in considering it merely as a temporary home, a sort of huge goose, out of which a few feathers were to be plucked, and then forsaken. It is for this reason that the life of the miner is at present tenfold more arduous than it otherwise would be, and never was there a more egregious error in regard to the character of the country. Gold is not the only product of the soil in California. Her fertile valleys and rich prairies are capable, when cultivated, of producing an untold store of agricultural wealth. Her lofty pines and spreading oak trees afford an abundant supply of material for the erection of comfortable dwellings. Her thousand streams, pouring down every hillside and winding through her plains, furnish an inexhaustible supply of water-power, and her forests, mountains, and lakes abound with game of every description. In the immense valleys of the Sacramento and San Joaquin, are millions of acres of land entirely unreclaimed, upon which any man may settle and make a fortune in a few years by the cultivation of the soil. Some hundred and fifty miles above Sacramento City, on the Sacramento River, are large tracts of valuable, well-watered land, much of which is unreclaimed, other portions being for sale at mere nominal prices. On one of these tracts, at "Lawson's Rancho," wheat was last year raised at an average of forty-five bushels to the acre, and is now selling delivered on the rancho at six dollars a bushel! Cattle bring from forty to a hundred dollars a head, potatoes twenty-five cents per pound, milk two dollars per gallon, butter from one to two dollars per pound, and every product of a farm is at corresponding prices. With the continued growth of California, the demand for all these articles, most of which are now brought from the Sandwich Islands, Chili, and Oregon, must necessarily increase, and I am satisfied that the cultivation of the soil will yet be a more profitable labour than extracting the gold from it.

California is a habitable country, and should be looked upon no longer as a mere temporary residence. A state government has been organized, the sheltering hand of law stretched over its borders, and life there can be made as comfortable as life in any other portion of the world. Let then the gold-digger come, and from the never-failing hills gather a rich supply of treasure. Let the farmer come, and from the abundant soil produce the necessaries of life, and enrich himself from them. Let the mechanic and labourer come, and build up the towns of this new country, and let the ladies of our land come, and with their smiles bring peace and happiness into the wilderness.

"The world was sad! the garden was a wild!
And man, the hermit sighed, till woman smiled!"

In this connexion, it may be well to state, that although California presents one of the finest fields in the world for mechanical and industrial pursuits, it is as yet an unpromising region for what are called "the learned professions;" and I would advise no more "of that ilk" to wend this way. The country is already overrun with young lawyers and doctors, who are too feeble physically to succeed as gold-diggers, and seek in vain for fees. Nearly all the law business done here is in the hands of a few prominent individuals, who are handsomely paid for what they do, but could readily transact ten times the amount of business that is ever placed in their hands. Public opinion is more stringent here than in the older states, and contracts are faithfully fulfilled, whether written or verbal, without evasion, under the technicalities or subtitles of the law. The medical profession is somewhat more in demand, but it is so crowded that few succeed, and most persons who come here to practise medicine, are compelled to resort to some other means of obtaining a livelihood. Hydropathy is the popular treatment, and a good bath is thought to be far more conducive to health than bleeding or calomel.

Using a rocker

CHAPTER XIII.

THE OLD TOWNS OF CALIFORNIA.

MONTEREY.

THE town of Monterey is situated upon the large bay of that name, formed by the curve of land between Point Ano Nuevo on the north, and Point Pinos on the south. Until the adoption of the present constitution for California, Monterey was always the seat of government of the territory, and the residence of her military governors and other officers. The town presents a very neat and pretty appearance, with its houses of white-plastered *adobes* and its surrounding hills covered with lofty pine trees. It retains its old Spanish peculiarities, and Yankee innovations have as yet made but little progress there. The Spanish *don,* clothed in his *serape* and *calcineros,* still walks through the streets with his lordly air, and the pretty *senorita,* her dark eyes peering through the folds of her *reboso,* skips lightly along the footpath. The ancient customs are still continued here, and the sound of the guitar and the light shuffling of pretty feet are heard nightly in the *casas.* I saw here a few weeks since a funeral celebrated in the old style, which, although by no means new to me, exceedingly astonished some Yankee friends who had but just arrived. A procession of some hundred people, men, women, and children, were straggling along the street, preceded by six little girls, dressed in white, bearing upon their shoulders the coffin of an infant. Upon one side of this were two musicians, with a guitar and violin, playing such tunes as are heard at the country dances in the United States, while upon the other were two tall fellows with muskets, which they were continually loading and firing. By the sides of the procession was a troop of boys, all armed with Chinese fire-crackers, which they exploded by the pack, keeping up a most infernal racket. In this manner the procession marched to the church, where the coffin was opened, and the little body strewn with wild flowers. After some Catholic ceremony the body was committed to the grave, when the whole posse adjourned to the residence of the parents, where a grand fandango and feast were given, which lasted throughout the whole night.

About six miles from Monterey lie the mission and valley of Carmel, one of the prettiest spots in all Upper California, and one of the most favourable for agricultural pursuits; and twenty-five miles distant is the great valley of San Juan, ten miles in width, and thirty miles in length. This valley possesses a climate peculiar to itself, and a soil of exceeding richness. The winds from the ocean are mellowed before they reach here, and fall with a delicious coolness upon this beautiful vale. The agricultural products are principally corn, wheat, and potatoes, which are taken to Monterey and sold at good prices.

The bay of Monterey abounds in fish of every variety, but particularly mackerel, which can be caught in great quantities with a hook and line directly in the harbour. The town contains about one thousand inhabitants, and its climate is superior to that of any other locality on the coast, although during the summer a dense fog usually rises for a few hours in the morning. A fort has been built upon a hill overlooking the town and harbour, and a military force is stationed there. There are several American residents in Monterey at the present time, engaged in mercantile pursuits; but very little building is in progress, and the town bids fair to remain for a long time a representative of California as she was before the indomitable Yankee introduced his "notions" into her territory.

SANTA BARBARA.

South of Monterey is the town of Santa Barbara, a place celebrated for its being the residence of the aristocracy of California, as well as for its beautiful women. There is no harbour to the town, and vessels are obliged to lie at anchor in an open roadstead, often at many miles distant from the shore; and during the spring and fall, when the southeast winds prevail, they are scarcely safe lying here; a high surf is constantly running on the beach, and it is only by the greatest skill in "beaching" a boat that one can escape a severe ducking. The position of the town of Santa Barbara is one of the most beautiful in California. On the right, toward the water, is a lofty hill, rising nearly a thousand feet, from the summit of which the little town resembles one of those mud villages, which school-boys mould in clam-shells. Directly back of the town is a range of almost impassable hills, which run in a diagonal direction, and join the Coast Range at San Luis Obispo. In front is the broad bay, embraced between two points, and having a smooth beach of nearly thirty miles in extent. A mile back from the town, at the head of a gentle slope, is the mission of Santa Barbara, with its venerable white walls and cross-mounted spires.

THE OLD TOWNS OF CALIFORNIA

The town itself is situated upon a plain of some ten miles in extent, and contains about one hundred and fifty houses, built of *adobes,* all one story in height. Most of these houses contain but two rooms, a large one called the *gala,* and a small chamber. These houses contain no stoves or fireplaces, all the cooking operations of a family being performed in the *cocina,* which is a building separate from the main dwelling.

The people of Santa Barbara are kind and hospitable. I was stationed there three months, and scarcely a day elapsed that our mess-table did not exhibit some choice specimen of California cookery, made up by the hands of some fair senorita, as a present to *"los officiales Americanos."* But here, as all over California, among the native population, laziness is the great characteristic of the people. A fine horse to ride, plenty of beef and *frijoles* to eat, and *cigaros* to smoke, and they are satisfied. The whole day with them is spent on horseback, in lazily riding from one tavern to another, or galloping furiously, at the risk of their necks, along the streets. The residents of Santa Barbara are principally *rancheros,* who visit their *ranchos* once or twice a year, to attend to the marking and killing of their cattle, and spend the remainder of the year in their town residence, enjoying life to their utmost capacity. Each *ranchero* usually keeps around the town a sufficient number of cattle for food, and whenever any beef is wanted, a bullock is slaughtered in a manner that would cause the eyes of the English societies for the suppression of cruelties to animals to stare aghast. The animal is first to be caught, which is effected in this manner. A *vaquero* or herdsman, mounted upon a fleet horse, and provided with a strong rope, with a noose at one end, and called a *lasso,* rides furiously into the herd of cattle, and selecting the one he wishes swings his lasso around his head, gives a loud yell, at the same time throwing the *lasso* and planting it over the horns and head of the vanquished bullock. So expert are they in the use of the *lasso* that they seldom fail at the first trial in catching an animal running at the distance of thirty or forty feet. The animal being captured, he is dragged into town, and being conducted within a *corral,* another lasso is thrown around his legs, which are thus tripped from under him, when a sharp knife is plunged into his throat.

The favourite amusement of the Californians is dancing, and Santa Barbara is more celebrated for its *fandangos* than any other town on the coast. These occur nearly every evening in the week, it being always easy to get up an impromptu ball in five minutes by calling in a guitar or harp player. At these balls there is no exclusiveness, the high and low, rich and poor, all meet on perfect equality, and dance away their sorrows, if they have any, upon the same mud floor. No scented cards of invitation are sent to the favoured few, but all who choose enter and participate freely. At church and at fandangos Californians all find a level. It appears as natural for Californians to dance as to breathe or eat. Often have I seen little girls, scarce six years of age, flying through a *cotillon,* or circling in the giddy waltz, or dancing with great skill their favourite *jotah* or *jarabe.* The girls are all elegant waltzers, and will exhaust the strength of an ordinary American gentleman, who is content with a few turns round the ball-room and then a long promenade.

The town of Santa Barbara contains about five hundred inhabitants, among whom are the Norrigas and Carillos, the two great families of California. It is a beautiful place of residence, with a mild, springlike climate, and around it are some of the pleasantest rides in all California. About four miles distant is the little town of *Montecito* (little mountain), a collection of farm-houses, where large quantities of vegetables are grown. Three miles beyond this in the heart of the mountains, is a remarkable hot sulphur spring, to which invalids resort for the purpose of bathing, and six miles in the opposite direction is an Indian village, containing some forty or fifty wigwams, whose tenants are an industrious agricultural people, who raise corn, wheat, and potatoes, and bring them into Santa Barbara for sale.

The mission of Santa Barbara is, at the present time, in a better condition than any other mission in the country. About fifty of the converted Indians still remain here and cultivate the soil. Around the old mission building are several extensive orchards, in which figs, apples, pears, and peaches are grown, and two or three vineyards, producing a grape from which excellent wine is made. *The Padre Presidente,* the presiding priest of California, resides here, the office at present devolving upon Padre Jesus Maria Gonzales, one of the kindest and most gentlemanly men I ever met with.

PUEBLO DE LOS ANGELOS.

One hundred and ten miles south of Santa Barbara is the *Pueblo de los Angelos* (City of the Angels), the garden spot of California. It is situated at the end of an immense plain, which extends from San Pedro, the port of the *Pueblo,* twenty-five miles distant, to this point. As in all California towns, the houses are built of *adobe* and are covered with an asphaltum, which is found in great quantities, issuing from the ground near the town. The northern portion of the town is laid out in streets, and appropriated as the residence of the trading citizens, while the southern part is made up of gardens, vineyards, and orchards. Through all these a large stream runs, which is used to irrigate the soil. The vineyards are lovely spots; acres upon acres of ground are covered with vines, which are trimmed every year, and thus kept about six feet in height, and in the fall of the year are hanging thick with clusters of grapes. In addition to these, apples, pears, peaches, plums, and figs are raised in great abundance. An American, named Wolfskill, has here a vineyard containing thirty thousand bearing grape-vines, from which he makes annually a thousand barrels of wine, and two or three hundred of *aguardiente,* the brandy of the country. Some of this wine is a very superior article, resembling in its flavour the best Madeira, while another kind, the *vino tinto,* is execrable stuff. With proper care and apparatus, however, the grape of the *Pueblo* could be made to yield as good wine as any in the world; and the whole plain, twenty-five miles in extent, reaching to the beach at San Pedro, is susceptible of the cultivation of the vine.

Until the late astonishing growth of San Francisco, the Pueblo was the largest town in California, containing about two thousand inhabitants, who are principally wealthy rancheros, and those who reside there to cultivate the grape. Game of many kinds abounds in the vicinity of the Pueblo. During the rainy season, the plains in the direction of San Pedro are covered with millions of geese and ducks, which are shot by the dozen, while the surrounding hills afford an abundance of quails, deer, elk, and antelope.

The inhabitants of the Pueblo are of the better and wealthier class of Californians, and have always been strongly disposed towards the institutions of Mexico, and at the time of the conquest of California, they fought with a determined resistance against the naval forces of Commodore Stockton. They have now, however, become reconciled to the institutions of our country, and will, I doubt not, in a few years make as good a set of democrats as can be found in Missouri or Arkansas. They are very strongly attached to the Roman Catholic Church, and are probably the most "religious," in their acceptation of the term, of any people in California. Every morning the solemn toll of the church-bell calls them to mass; at noon it is rung again, and every Poblano at the sound doffs his sombrero, and remains reverently uncovered in the hot sun, while the bell reminds him that he is to utter a short prayer. In whatever avocation they may be engaged, whether fiddling, dancing, singing, slaughtering cattle, or playing billiards or monte, the custom is invariably followed. I have seen a party in a tavern in the Pueblo, busily engaged in betting against a monte bank, when the noonday bell tolled; a fellow, with his last dollar in the world placed upon a card, immediately doffed his hat and muttered his prayer; the dealer laid down his cards and did the same, and they continued in their humble positions till the bell ceased tolling, when the game and the swearing went on as busily as usual.

About ten miles from Los Angelos, is the mission of San Gabriel, located upon the river of that name, whose banks for miles are girdled with grape-vines. This is one of the prettiest spots in California, and affords a fine opportunity for the raising of fruit. The country around the Pueblo is by far the most favourable portion of southern California for the settlement of foreigners. Possessing a climate of unequalled mildness, and a soil of great fertility, it must inevitably, ere long, be surrounded by a large population.

SAN DIEGO.

The town of San Diego is the southernmost of Upper California, the boundary line established by the late treaty running one marine league south of it. The harbour here, next to that at San Francisco, is the best on the whole coast, perfectly land-locked, protected from the gales at all seasons of the year, and the entrance is so narrow that but one vessel can pass through at the same time. A vessel can lie within a cable's length of the beach, which is of hard sand, and upon which no surf runs. The town itself lies three miles from the beach, is about the size of Santa Barbara, and is overlooked by an old Mexican fortress. San Diego has always been the greatest depot for hides upon the coast; the facilities for taking them from the shore to the vessel being greater than at any other point. The climate is mild and pleasant; and the town is rapidly growing, and bids fair to become of great commercial importance. An immense inland trade will be carried on from this place with the settlements that must arise on the Colorado and Gila rivers, and around the head of the Gulf of California. The country in its immediate vicinity is well adapted for grazing, and abounds in wild game.

CHAPTER XIV.

THE NEW TOWNS OF CALIFORNIA.

THE enormous price of real estate in San Francisco, and the continual rapid tide of emigration, will ere long cause the settlement of the new towns seated at various points in the vicinity of the mining region. Many of these are entirely new, but have grown and are growing with great rapidity. I propose giving a description of their locations as a guide to those who may desire to settle in any of them.

BENICIA.

The town or city of Benicia, which in the king's English means Venice, is situated in the straits of Carquinez, thirty-five miles from San Francisco, which it promises yet to rival in point of commercial importance. The ground upon which it is seated is a gentle slope descending to the water, and as it reaches it becoming almost a plain. There is sufficient water at its bank to enable vessels of the first class to lie at anchor there, and discharge their cargoes, and the harbour is safe and exempt from violent winds. Benicia contains already about a thousand inhabitants, including a garrison of soldiers, having been made the head-quarters of the Pacific division of the United States Army. The large deposits of quartermaster's stores have been removed from San Francisco to Benicia, and a site has been selected by Commodore Jones for a navy-yard at this point. The town was originally laid out some three years since by Robert Semple and Thomas O. Larkin. Lots of fifty varas square are selling at from five hundred to two thousand dollars.

MARTINEZ.

The town of Martinez is also located on the straits of Carquinez, nearly opposite Benicia. The site of the town is pleasant, being upon a high bank, while the plain around it is well wooded. The proprietor is William M. Smith of San Francisco, who is making arrangements for building the town.

SIX MONTHS IN THE GOLD MINES

NEW YORK OF THE PACIFIC.

At the junction of the river San Joaquin and the bay of Suisun, lies New York of the Pacific. The town is seated on a broad and well-watered plain, covered with many groves of magnificent oaks, extending from the waters of the bay and the river San Joaquin to the hills some three miles back. So gradual is the slope that it seems a perfect level, viewed from the river's bank; but standing at the base of the hills looking toward the water, the slope will be found to be perfect and regular to the water's edge, where it terminates upon a fine sand-beach, from five to ten feet above the level of the highest tide. New York is beautifully laid out, with large reserves for churches, a university, and other public edifices, and is perhaps one of the most healthy points in the country, being free from fever and ague and the prevailing fevers usual on fresh-water rivers below and between the mining region and San Francisco. But the great advantage which New York of the Pacific possesses over other places above San Francisco is, that it is at the head of ship navigation, as two regular surveys, published by distinguished military and naval officers of Suisun Bay have demonstrated. Ships of the largest class can sail direct from the ocean to New York, where they will find a safe and convenient harbour, and where at this time are lying a number of merchant ships from different parts of the Union, directly alongside the bank upon which they have discharged their cargoes.

New York is surrounded on all sides by the most fertile agricultural districts of Northern California. The Sacramento, San Joaquin, and San Jose valleys being tributary to this point which is as the centre of so many radii, while the entire land travel from San Jose and the Contra Costa, and indeed of all southern California, flows through this channel. The whole transportation to the rich placers of the Stanislaus, Mokelumne, Tuolumne, Merced, and Mariposa, as well as the famous mines of the Middle, North, and South Forks, Feather and Yuba rivers, must pass the new city. The great railroad, destined to connect the Pacific Ocean and the Mississippi River, will undoubtedly terminate at New York, as it is in a direct line with the only pass in the mountains through which a railroad can reach the waters which empty into the Bay of San Francisco. This is a fact well established by the most distinguished engineers. Through the enterprise of Col. J. D. Stevenson and Dr. William C. Parker, both of the New York regiment of volunteers, the first survey of the bay of Suisun and the adjacent waters was

THE NEW TOWNS OF CALIFORNIA

made. These gentlemen are the principal owners of New York.

SUISUN.

The city of "Suisun," alluded to in the first chapter of this narrative under the cognomen of Hala-chum-muck, is laid out on the west bank of the Sacramento, at a distance of eighty miles from San-Francisco, and is about half-way between San Francisco and Sacramento City. The town is seated on high ground, and is entirely free from the *tule,* a rush that grows upon the marshy banks of the river. It is beautifully laid out, with large reserves for churches, a university, and other public edifices, and the beauty of its climate and surrounding scenery will eventually make it a favourable and pleasant place of residence. The proprietors are Thomas Douglass and C. V. Gillespie. Lots are selling at from $250 to $800.

SUTTER.

The city of Sutter is beautifully located on the eastern bank of the Sacramento River, adjoining Sacramento City, and is perhaps the most eligible site for a commercial town in all Northern California. It is situated on the highest and healthiest ground on the whole river, the banks at this point not being subject to the annual overflow. The largest class of steamboats and all vessels navigating the Sacramento River, can lie and discharge their cargoes directly at its banks.

Sutter was originally laid out by Captain J. A. Sutter and others, but has not until recently been brought forward by its proprietors. It has, however, a thriving business population, and promises to become a city of the first size and importance. Excellent roads diverge from this point to the rich placers of the North, Middle, and South Forks, Bear River, Yuba, and Feather Rivers, and also to the mines of the San Joaquin. It is surrounded on all sides by a fine agricultural and well-wooded country, and will soon be the depot for the great northern mines. Its present proprietors are the Hon. John M'Dougal, Lieutenant-Governor of the State of California, and Captain J. A. Sutter.

VERNON.

Vernon is situated on the east bank of Feather River at the point of its confluence with the Sacramento, one of the most eligible positions for a town in the whole northern region of California. The banks of the river are high and not subject to overflow, and this point is said to be at the head of ship navigation on the Sacramento. The ground is a gentle slope, surrounded by a beautiful country. From the town of Vernon, good and well travelled roads diverge to the rich mineral regions of the North and Middle Forks, Bear Creek, Yuba and Feather Rivers, rendering the distance much less than by any other route. The town is growing rapidly, and promises to become a great depot for the trade of the above-mentioned mines. The proprietors are Franklin Bates, Elisha O. Crosby, and Samuel Norriss.

BOSTON.

The city of Boston is located on the northern bank of the American Fork, at its junction with the Sacramento River, about one hundred yards above the old *Embarcadero,* the site upon which Sacramento City now stands. It extends upon the banks of both rivers for several miles, and is destined to become a flourishing town. The banks of the Sacramento at this point are not subject to overflow, being more than twelve feet in many places above high water mark. The town is situated upon a broad and well-watered plain, covered with many groves of magnificent oaks, and the largest class of steamers, and all vessels navigating the Sacramento River can lie and discharge directly at its banks.

Boston has been surveyed by J. Halls, Esq., and Lieut. Ringgold, U. S. N., and is laid out in squares of two hundred and forty feet by three hundred and twenty feet, subdivided each into eight building lots eighty feet by one hundred and twenty feet, with large public squares, and reservations for school-houses, churches, and public buildings. One of the peculiar advantages of Boston is that, being located on the northern bank of the American Fork, it is not necessary in proceeding to the gold mines to cross that river, which is exceedingly high and rapid at some seasons of the year. The direct and most travelled road proceeds from this point to the rich placers of the Yuba, Feather River, Bear Creek, and the North, Middle, and South Forks of the American. The soil is of the richest description, the surrounding scenery highly picturesque, and the plains in the immediate vicinity are covered with wild game of every variety which California affords. The title to the land is indisputable, coming by warranty deed from Captain

THE NEW TOWNS OF CALIFORNIA

J. A. Sutter to Eleab Grimes, Hiram Grimes, and John Sinclair, bearing date August 10th, 1843. The present owner is Hiram Grimes, Esq. Lots are selling rapidly at from $200 to $1000 each, and before many months the city of Boston on the golden banks of the Rio Sacramento will rival its New England namesake in business and importance.

STOCKTON.

The town of Stockton is the great mart through which flows the whole transportation and travel to the placers of the Stanislaus, Mokelumne, Mariposa, Mercedes, Tuolumne, and King's River, and the various dry diggings lying between them. Stockton is to the southern mines what Sacramento is to the northern. The town is located upon a slough, or rather a succession of sloughs, which contain the back waters formed by the junction of the Sacramento and San Joaquin rivers. It is about fifty miles from the mouth of the San Joaquin, and one hundred from San Francisco. The ground is high and does not overflow, and is the centre of the two great tracts of arable land which constitute the valleys of the rivers above named. Vessels drawing from nine to ten feet of water can proceed up the San Joaquin to Stockton, and discharge their cargoes on the bank.

The town of Stockton was laid out in the latter part of 1848 by Charles M. Weber, and has been growing rapidly since. Eight months ago there were but one frame building and a few tents, and now it is a town containing a population of nearly two thousand permanent residents, and a movable population of about a thousand more, on their way to and from the southern mines. Several large brigs and schooners are constantly lying at the banks, and two steamboats and a large number of launches are constantly running from San Francisco. Real estate has risen greatly in value within the past six months, —lots, which could have been purchased at that time for $300, being now worth from $3000 to $6000. A theatre has been established at Stockton, and the town promises ere long to be a large and populous city.

STANISLAUS.

This town is laid out on the north bank of the Stanislaus River, at its junction with the San Joaquin. The Stanislaus River is the first and largest tributary of the San Joaquin, and the river is navigable for ordinary-sized schooners and launches to this point, which, being nearer the southern mining region than Stockton, will doubtless become a great resort for miners and traders in that vicinity. The town was originally laid out by Samuel Brannan & Co.

SOUTH SAN FRANCISCO

The city of South San Francisco is located on the bay, about two miles south of San Francisco, which it promises to rival at no very distant day. The depth of water at this point is the same as that in the harbour of San Francisco, and it is said that vessels are more securely protected from the wind. At many points in front of the town, vessels of the largest class can lie within a boat's length of the shore. The land rises in a gentle slope, and is of a rich clayey soil, which effectually prevents dust during the prevalence of the customary winds on the bay. The surrounding scenery is delightful, and near the town is the rich and beautiful valley in which is located the old mission of *Dolores*. A stream of fine water, sufficient to supply all the shipping in the harbour, runs through the town, and the only practicable road from San Francisco to San Jose, Monterey, and the whole lower country, passes directly by it. South San Francisco, though it may never equal its northern namesake, will at least become, at no very distant day, what Brooklyn is to New York. The proprietors of South San Francisco are John Townsend and Corneille De Boom.

ALVESO

The want of a great commercial town at the head of the great bay of San Francisco has been supplied by the location of Alveso. It is situated at the head of the bay, on the Guadalupe River, a stream running directly through the centre of the town, and navigable at all seasons of the year to vessels drawing twelve feet of water. The depot and business headquarters of the two finest valleys in California, the Santa Clara and the Pueblo, where everything required for their already numerous population must be received; convenient of access to the gold mines, and directly on the route between them and San Francisco; with a climate unequalled, even in Upper California; with pure water; free from inundations at all seasons; with mills which even now furnish lumber at one-third its price in San Francisco,—the

Robert Semple,
Proprietor of Benicia

town of Alveso must inevitably grow into importance. It has been carefully surveyed and laid out into lots; contracts have been made for the immediate erection of warehouses and dwellings, and a bridge is now being built across the Guadalupe River, connecting the two portions of the town. The proprietors are J. D. Koppe, Peter H. Burnett, and Charles B. Marvin, who will doubtless reap a rich harvest, the fruits of their judicious enterprise.

Thomas O. Larkin
Proprietor of Benicia

CHAPTER XV.

LOWER CALIFORNIA

THE territory of Lower California (California Baja) has been so much misrepresented, that although partially foreign to the object of this work, I consider it may not be uninteresting to learn something of a country which, I am satisfied, will one day create almost as much excitement in the old world as her northern sister has already done. A residence of six months upon the gulf of California entirely changed the opinion I had previously entertained of the country, which had been based upon reports of those who had merely sailed up or down its rugged coast. It has been described as the "tail end of an earthquake,"—as possessing a soil upon which nothing could be grown, a hot and sickly climate, and containing no internal resources of value.

Lower California extends from Cape St. Lucas to a line running one marine league south of San Diego, being bounded on the west by the Pacific Ocean, and on the east by the gulf of California. I went to Lower California in the full anticipation of living a miserable life for the time it would be necessary for me to remain there. But how much was I surprised, on landing in La Paz, on the afternoon of July 21st, 1847, to find the prettiest town I had then seen in California. The streets were lined with willow trees, which, meeting overhead, formed an arch, affording a delicious shade at midday. The houses were all of *adobe,* plastered white, and thatched with the leaves of the palm-tree, and were most delightfully cool. The whole beach was lined with palms, date, fig, tamarind, and cocoanut trees, their delicious fruits hanging upon them in clusters.

The detachment of the 7th regiment of New York Volunteers, which was ordered to La Paz, consisted of two companies, "A" and "B," under command of Lieut. Col. Henry S. Burton. When we arrived, we found that country in a quiet state; and although no American force had ever been stationed there, the inhabitants appeared very much pleased at our arrival, and manifested no hostility toward us. Our orders were to take possession of, and hold the country; and in accordance with these we landed, and pitched our camp in the plaza, previous to removing into a large barrack, which was not then quite completed. When our men were fairly barracked, the officers were allowed to live in rooms in the town, and select such places as they chose. I found a room in the house of Don Francisco Silva, a Portuguese, who had lived long in the country, and owned the finest vineyard and fruit-garden in the town. Here I lived in a style of Eastern luxuriance. Never before did I, and never shall I desire to enjoy life in greater perfection than I did there. My room was in the rear of the house, and fronting upon a garden filled with grape-vines, fig, orange, lime, banana, and pomegranate trees, loaded with fruit. I slept in a swinging cot, surrounded by a silken canopy, as a protection from mosquitoes; and often have I taken my cot, swung it before the limbs of a large fig-tree, and slept beneath that clear, unclouded sky, rocked to slumber by the delightful evening land-breeze. In the morning, before breakfast, I would pick from the limbs and eat a few dozens of ripe, fresh figs, by way of giving me an appetite. But the most delicious portion of this delicious life was the bathing. In the centre of the garden was a large stone reservoir, kept continually filled with water, and used for the purpose of irrigation. Into this I would jump at noon, and, standing upon the stony bottom, could gather big clusters of grapes, hanging upon an arbour that overspread the whole bath. Our military duties were so light that they never interfered with this pleasant mode of life, particularly as our commanding officer was not very strict in his enforcement of them, and the reveille drum seldom disturbed my morning slumbers.

If an epicure wishes to enjoy life at a low rate, I advise him to go to Lower California. The Gulf affords every variety of fish, and all the tropical fruits grow in the greatest profusion. For several months we lived upon green turtle, caught directly in front of the town,—some of them weighed one hundred and fifty pounds, and were sold to us at twenty-five cents apiece. In addition to this, the shores afforded mussels and oysters in great plenty, and the soil produces every variety of vegetables. Among the fruits of Lower California is one which grows wild, and is peculiar to the country, called the *petalla,* the most delicious fruit I ever ate. It grows upon a kind of cactus tree, and somewhat resembles a prickly pear, being covered with a thorny rind, which, being taken off, exhibits a pulp of a rich red colour. The great peculiarity of this fruit is, that out of a hundred no two have the same flavour. One resembles in taste a strawberry; another, seems flavoured with winter-green; the next with peach, and so on through the whole range of cultivated fruits.

LOWER CALIFORNIA

The climate of Lower California is equal to that of Italy or Persia. During the whole year, the thermometer never varies ten degrees, usually ranging from eighty to ninety degrees, except at noon, when it sometimes reaches one hundred. In the winter, no other than thin clothing is worn, and an overcoat is never needed. It is an eternal summer. Such gorgeous sunsets and clear star-lit skies, can be found in no other portion of the world. During my whole residence there, I never saw a cloud as large as my hand upon the sky, and a drop of rain never fell. There is no rainy season in Lower California; rain usually falls three or four times in the course of a year, but the necessity of it is almost superseded by the heavy dews which fall every night.

The healthiness of the country is remarkable. During our sojourn there of more than a year, no death from sickness occurred in our detachment of more than a hundred men, and but two deaths during the whole time in the town, which consisted of fifteen hundred inhabitants. An officer of our regiment who was stationed in Upper California, and who had been pronounced by his physicians to be in the last stage of pulmonary consumption, as a last resort went to Lower California. The result was, that in three months he completely regained his health, and I saw him a few days since a stout, hearty man.

The people of Lower California are a curious race of beings; isolated from their mother country and neglected by her, they have assumed a sort of independence of thought and action which I never found in Upper California; but a kinder-hearted, more hospitable class of people never lived. Their thatched houses are ever open for the reception of visitors, and a glass of wine and a paper cigar are always offered to any one who chooses to enter. The manner in which the people of La Paz live is peculiar. In the main street, the houses are built of *adobe,* whitewashed, with roofs principally of cane and palm-tree, laid flat and covered with the shell of the pearl oyster. Some of them are of more than one story in height. Some of the floors are laid with large square bricks, but by far the greater portion of them are of the native mud. In the interior arrangement, little attention is paid to decoration. A few camp-stools covered with leather, or a drum-shaped seat with a piece of raw hide drawn over it, a table, a bed, and an earthen jar filled with water, usually compose the furniture. The bed is usually very neat, with clean linen sheets and curtains, with red satin covered pillows. In the other parts of the town and on the outskirts, the houses are very small, some of them of *adobe,* others of reeds, plastered with mud, and others are nothing more than a parcel of dried bushes intertwined. These generally contain but one room, with no more furniture than a few seats, and sometimes a bed made of a dried hide tightly drawn across four posts. Here father, mother, daughters, and sons, all lie down promiscuously on a hide stretched upon the floor, or, more commonly still, outside in the open air, and sleep heads and points in most admirable confusion. Indeed, this sleeping out of doors is not confined to any particular class, but is practised by all during the summer months, and is really a delightful mode of passing the night. The men are generally tall and well-formed, and dress in the manner of Mexicans of the same class.

But the women, "Heaven's last, best work," how shall I describe them? They are found in Lower California of all shades, from the blackest ebony to the whitest lily. Where such a variety of colour could have arisen, I cannot imagine. Their dress is usually a skirt, merely reaching to the waist, while above this, is a white bodice which does not reach quite so high in the neck as is required by the strict rules of feminine modesty. They wear no hats or bonnets, but in lieu of them a *reboso* is thrown around their heads, and falls in graceful folds over their shoulders. Many of them go barefoot, and very few wear stockings, considering them an unnecessary luxury.

Simple as are these articles of dress, the La Paz girls delight as much as their more refined sisters in our northern cities in exhibiting themselves to advantage. I have seen a fair senorita on her way to church, as barefooted as the day she first trod the earth, carrying on her shoulders a beautiful silk *reboso*, which must have cost a hundred dollars. The ladies all indulge in the "amiable weakness" of smoking cigaritos, and the blue wreaths are curling about their dark faces from morning to night. The state of morals amongst them is as loose as their dress, and the poorer classes are sunk in the lowest state of prostitution. Cases have often occurred where the bargain for the daughter's dishonour has previously been made with the mother. Strange as this may appear in a country upon which the light of Christianity has shone, and among a people professing to be Christian, it is, nevertheless, strictly true.

In fact the morals of the whole community, male and female, need improving. An old priest named Gabriel, who, at the time I was there, was Padre Presidente of Lower California, in open violation of his vows of chastity, was living in the family relation, and had been the means of bringing into the world no less than eleven children. One of these had taken his name, always travelled with him, and was himself studying for the priesthood. I witnessed a very amusing incident once with Gabriel, in which I bore a part, and which exhibits the peculiar state of morals among some of the priesthood of Mexican territory. Gabriel was a most inveterate gambler, and often amused himself, when on his parochial tours, by opening a game of monte for any of his parishioners who chose to bet against him, although he often found difficulty in obtaining a game, because, as the "knowing ones" said, "El padre sabe mucho."

Soon after our arrival at La Paz, Gabriel, who resided in Todos Santos, came over to visit his flock in La Paz, and as we were then the lions of the place, he invited the officers to visit him at his temporary residence in the town. Soon after we entered, when he had brought out a bottle of good old wine, he very quietly took from a pocket in his cassock a pack of monte cards, and asked us if we had any objection to a quiet game. Out of courtesy we told him that we had no objection, and the padre commenced dealing and we betting.

After our amusement had been in progress about half an hour, during which time the padre had beaten us to the amount of a few dollars, the bell of the church tolled. The padre laid down his cards and said with perfect *nonchalance:* "Dispensame Senores, tengo que bautizar un niño." (Excuse me, gentlemen, I have a child to baptize.) He invited us to proceed to the church with him, and when we arrived, we found a woman with a child anxiously waiting in the doorway. When, however, the padre was ready to commence operations, it was found that there was no one present to stand in the capacity of *compadre* (godfather). Gabriel invited me to perform this service. I told him I was not a Catholic. "No le hace," was his reply; and I accordingly stood at the baptismal font while the padre sprinkled the youngster and muttered over some Latin, after which, he turned to my companions and myself, and said, "Ahora, Senores, vamos a jugar otra vez." (Now, gentlemen, we will go and play again); and we accordingly returned to the house and resumed the game. Gabriel was afterwards taken prisoner by our forces and sent to Mazatlan. He was one of the leading spirits in the revolution that afterwards occurred, and I doubt not that he came to La Paz, at the time of which I have spoken, to learn our force, and the probabilities of our being taken.

Among such a people, ignorant but kind, and in such a glorious climate, I passed my days in happiness and pleasure. When the shades of evening gathered around us, a little knot of us used to assemble beneath a spreading tamarind tree, and listen to songs in the enchanting Spanish, sung by a beautiful creature who had undertaken the task of teaching me her language, and in which, I flatter myself, she found an apt scholar. A ramble then upon the broad, hard beach, beneath that beautiful starlight, would close our evening's pleasures, or a dance upon a greensward in a grove of fig-trees, prepare us for a sweet slumber.

Sometimes we took little excursions upon the broad and placid bay, and one of these, which extended to a visit to the Pearl Fishery, I will relate: On a clear, beautiful, moonlit night, in the latter part of October, a party of three of us, in a little fishing-boat, stood out from the Bay of La Paz, to proceed to the Pearl Fishery of San Lorenzo, about twenty miles distant. We chose the night, for its coolness, and for the delicious land breeze which blew our little boat so rapidly over the water, and afforded so pleasing a contrast in feeling to the burning sun and stirless atmosphere of a tropical climate.

To one who has never been buoyed on the waters of the Gulf of California, no description can convey an accurate idea of its stillness and beauty, when, at the close of the long, sunny day, it is resting beneath the smile of the unclouded, starry sky, which is ever above it. Like a little inland lake in summer-time, unrippled and mirror-like, its waters were so clear that, even by moonlight, its shell-paved bottom was plainly discernible. Millions of little emerald-coloured gems of phosphorescent light, were floating over its bosom; and the track of the leaping porpoises and golden dolphins was followed by a stream of liquid fire.

As we neared "Pichelingo," the entrance to the harbour, we observed on the beach, about a mile distant, a bright light, and as the land breeze was dying away, we made for it, thinking that probably a party of divers were there, on their way to the fishery. We stood in, and soon reached the light, which we found to be a fire built on shore. We landed, hauled up our boat, and found two tall, naked Indians, engaged in cooking their evening meal of *pozzoli*, or boiled corn: they were tortoise-shell fishers, and had with them a large quantity of these most beautiful shells. They invited us to participate in their frugal meal, but we had provisions of our own, and, roasting some salt pork on their fire and brewing a steaming hot punch, we ate and drank sufficiently, spread our blankets on the sand and lay down to sleep by the side of our Indian friends. At daylight a good breeze sprang up, and, thanking our Indians for their hospitality and presenting each with a small sum of money, we again made sail.

LOWER CALIFORNIA

About 11 o'clock we rounded the low, sandy point, which forms one side of the entrance to the pretty little bay of San Lorenzo. We were received on the beach by about three hundred tall, black-looking Indians, prepared to start on their daily occupation of diving. Through the politeness of one of the "armadores," or owners, six of the *busos* (divers) were placed in our boat, and we pushed off for the fishing-ground, near the shore of the huge rocky island of Espiritu Santo. Thirty canoes, filled with divers, started with us, and in half an hour we were on the ground. Here the water was the most beautifully clear I ever saw. It was some four or five fathoms in depth, but so transparent that the pearly treasures in its bed were as plain to our sight as though air only separated them from us. The divers divested themselves of every particle of clothing, with the exception of a girdle tightly bound round their loins, and armed with nothing but a sharp-pointed stick, about a foot in length used for the double purpose of fighting sharks and digging up the shell, they commenced their labours. Starting up suddenly on the gunwale of the boat, and giving a shrill whistle, to expel the air from their lungs, with a dive as graceful as a dolphin's leap, they plunged into the water, and made a straight course for the bottom. The dive itself carried them about two fathoms downward, and every subsequent stroke one fathom. Arrived at the bottom, they commenced digging up the shell, and each one soon returned to the surface with an armful, which he threw into the boat, and then would dive again for a fresh load, and so they continued for nearly three hours, with scarcely a moment's intermission. Some brought up fish and sea-weed, others beautiful shells, and one fellow captured a small shark, which he threw into the boat, very much to the annoyance of us landsmen.

These divers are Indians from the Slake River, in the province of Sonora, who come every season to the coast of California to pursue their avocation. About three o'clock the whole fleet started for the shore, and, arrived there, each buso carried his pile of shell on the beach, and the crew of each boat, forming a circle, threw into its centre one-half of their shells. These were the property of the *armador,* and were first opened, and the pearls given to him. The old fellow stood by, watching the divers very closely, as some of them are exceedingly expert in suddenly swallowing any valuable pearl they may chance to find in the owner's pile. The pearls are found in the body of the oyster, of all sizes, from that of a pin's head to that of a walnut. Sometimes a hundred oysters are opened without finding a single pearl, while in others many are found. When the owner's oysters are all opened, each diver commences on his own pile; and any valuable pearl he may find is usually sold to the *armador* on the spot, at about one-half its real value.

The pearl fisheries of Lower California have been carried on since the earliest discovery of the country, and immense fortunes have been made in them. There are at present about one hundred vessels yearly engaged in this business during the fishing season, which continues from May to November. The oysters are all taken by diving, no scientific apparatus having yet been successfully introduced. A diving-bell was tried by an English company some years ago, but this mode was soon abandoned, from some cause which I could never learn. The shells of the oysters are piled up on the beach, and sold to whalers and trading vessels that visit the coast.

The oysters being all opened, the divers take their first meal in the day, which consists of nothing more than a bowl of *atole,* a kind of water-gruel, with a little dried meat thrown into it. This, and the use of the boats, is all that is furnished by the *armador,* for which he receives one-half the pearls.

It was the last day of the fishing season, and before we left, as was always the custom, the little brush houses, temporarily thrown up on the beach, were fired by the divers, and a general jubilee held. We left them in the most glorious state of intoxication, and setting sail once more, after spending another night on the beach of Pichelingo, we arrived safely in La Paz the next day at noon.

The great resources of Lower California are its mines of silver, gold, copper, and iron, the former metal being most abundant. The whole mountain range, which extends along the coast, is one immense silver mine, equal in richness to those of Mexico or Peru. At the present time only three or four mines are wrought, owing to the lack of energy in the inhabitants, and the entire absence of scientific mining apparatus, — all the necessary labour being performed by men and mules. In making inquiries for a place to search for silver in Lower California, the old settlers in reply merely point their fingers to the mountain range, and say, "Por hay" (that way, anywhere there); and it is a fact, that a shaft may be sunk in any part of the mountains, and silver ore always extracted, varying in richness from fifteen to seventy per cent of pure silver. The principal silver mines at present wrought are in San Antonio, halfway from La Paz to Cape St. Lucas. These are owned by the Hidalgos, who send annually out of the country about two hundred thousand dollars worth of *plata pina*.

LOWER CALIFORNIA

Near Loretto are large and extensive copper mines; lead and iron are found everywhere, and gold-washings have always been wrought in the country with considerable success. If this territory ever becomes settled by an energetic population, millions of wealth will be annually gathered in its borders, and it will stand side by side in point of riches with the countries that have already made themselves famous by the wealth lying in their bosoms.

As an agricultural country Lower California is rather deficient, although there are many watered valleys which produce in great profusion all the common culinary vegetables, and wherever the soil can be irrigated, it produces all the tropical fruits and the vegetables of the temperate zones in great luxuriance. Cotton of the finest staple grows wild upon the plains around La Paz, and cane, from which a very good article of sugar is made, grows all over the land. Wine is made from the grape of the country, which is of the most delicious kind.

When we went to Lower California, our orders were to assure the inhabitants that their country was to be retained as a portion of the territory of the United States. The message of President Polk and the proclamation of Commodore Shubrick supported this idea, and upon the representations thus made, the most influential inhabitants committed themselves to the American cause, and were exceedingly gratified with the expected result. In the month of November, we were attacked by a Mexican force of six hundred, under command of Don Manuel Pineda, a captain in the Mexican army, who published a long proclamation threatening death and destruction to the Californians who supported our cause. Notwithstanding this, during a severe and trying siege, which lasted six weeks, many of the *rancheros* from the interior came in and joined us, and for this whole time a company of native Californians, under the command, of the former governor of the territory, Don Francisco Palaceo, fought bravely with us and rendered us essential service, with the expectation that at the close of the war they would be protected by us. But what was their consternation when, upon the reception of the news of the treaty of peace, it was found that they had been forgotten, and that after the promises which had been made, we were obliged to desert them and leave them to the voracity of their Mexican masters, by whom they are now of course viewed in the light of traitors to their country.

Never in the history of wars among civilized nations was there a greater piece of injustice committed, and the United States government deserves for it the imprecations of all who have a sense of justice remaining in them. The probability is, that some ignorant scribbler, who had cast his eyes upon the rugged rocks that girdle her sea-coast, had represented Lower California as a worthless country, and that, forgetting justice and good faith, our government left this compromised people to suffer at the hands of their own brethren. The result was that many of them were obliged to fly from their country and go to Upper California, their property was confiscated and they can never return to their homes but with the brand of traitors resting upon them.

It is the duty of our government to repair if possible the wrong thus done. Lower California must at some time inevitably be a territory of the United States. It is a peculiarity of the Yankee race that, like the western farmer, they only want to possess "all the land that joins them;" and this country, isolated as it is from Mexico, inhabited by a people who heartily hate the institutions of their mother country, neglected by her, and lying in such close contiguity to our possessions on the Pacific coast, must fall into our hands, and, instead of being a worthless territory, we should find it our greatest acquisition on the Pacific. The gulf of California is one of the finest sheets of water in the world, and the inner coast is indented with many safe and land-locked harbours. The bay of La Paz is safe and large, and the establishment of a naval depot at this point would keep in check the whole western coast of Mexico. Mexico does not desire this territory, and no people were ever more anxious for a separation from the mother country than are the inhabitants of Lower California. It would be an easy purchase, and if necessary an easy conquest, and unless it is done by the general government, a second Texas affair will occur there before many years pass. When Upper California becomes more thickly populated, and the progress westward is stopped by the surges of the Pacific, the northern territory of Oregon being already ours, the progress must inevitably be southward, and even now ideas are entertained of seizing the country.

In order to prevent the disastrous consequences which must ensue from a re-enaction of the Texas tragedies, and to render justice to a people whose confidence has been abused by our government, I would respectfully recommend to the home government the immediate commencement of negotiations for the purchase of this valuable and interesting territory. The appointment of commissioners to report upon its resources and its value in a naval point of view, would be speedily followed by its purchase, and thus would be prevented the piratical expeditions for the seizure of the country

LOWER CALIFORNIA

which otherwise will soon be undertaken.

THE END.

Printed in the United States
5347